BUSINESS ISSUES, COMPETITION AND ENTREPRENEURSHIP

SMALL BUSINESS HEALTH INSURANCE

COVERAGE AND TAX INCENTIVE ANALYSES

BUSINESS ISSUES, COMPETITION AND ENTREPRENEURSHIP

Additional books in this series can be found on Nova's website under the Series tab.

Additional E-books in this series can be found on Nova's website under the E-book tab.

HEALTH CARE ISSUES, COSTS AND ACCESS

Additional books in this series can be found on Nova's website under the Series tab.

Additional E-books in this series can be found on Nova's website under the E-book tab.

SMALL BUSINESS HEALTH INSURANCE

COVERAGE AND TAX INCENTIVE ANALYSES

IBRAHIM N. MCCORMICK
EDITOR

publishers
New York

Copyright © 2013 by Nova Science Publishers, Inc.

For permission to use material from this book please contact us:
Telephone 631-231-7269; Fax 631-231-8175
Web Site: http://www.novapublishers.com

NOTICE TO THE READER

The Publisher has taken reasonable care in the preparation of this book, but makes no expressed or implied warranty of any kind and assumes no responsibility for any errors or omissions. No liability is assumed for incidental or consequential damages in connection with or arising out of information contained in this book. The Publisher shall not be liable for any special, consequential, or exemplary damages resulting, in whole or in part, from the readers' use of, or reliance upon, this material. Any parts of this book based on government reports are so indicated and copyright is claimed for those parts to the extent applicable to compilations of such works.

Independent verification should be sought for any data, advice or recommendations contained in this book. In addition, no responsibility is assumed by the publisher for any injury and/or damage to persons or property arising from any methods, products, instructions, ideas or otherwise contained in this publication.

This publication is designed to provide accurate and authoritative information with regard to the subject matter covered herein. It is sold with the clear understanding that the Publisher is not engaged in rendering legal or any other professional services. If legal or any other expert assistance is required, the services of a competent person should be sought. FROM A DECLARATION OF PARTICIPANTS JOINTLY ADOPTED BY A COMMITTEE OF THE AMERICAN BAR ASSOCIATION AND A COMMITTEE OF PUBLISHERS.

Additional color graphics may be available in the e-book version of this book.

Library of Congress Cataloging-in-Publication Data

ISBN: 978-1-62417-239-7

Published by Nova Science Publishers, Inc. † New York

CONTENTS

PREFACE

This book offers an overview of the issues and status of small business health insurance in the United States and examines the question of whether existing tax incentives at the Federal and State level provide sufficient inducement to small businesses to adopt health insurance plans for their employees. Also discussed is the small business health insurance tax credit which was adopted as part of the Federal health care reform legislation and the factors contributing to its low use and complexity.

Chapter 1 – In the United States, most people get health insurance either through their employer or through a spouse's or parent's employer. According to the most recent estimates of the Current Population Survey (CPS), March 2010 Supplement, 55.8 percent of the U.S. population have access to health insurance through an employer, 30.6 percent have access to health insurance through a government program (such as Medicare, Medicaid, or SCHIP), 8.9 percent privately purchase health insurance on their own, and 16.7 percent are uninsured.

Historically, there have been distinct advantages to obtaining health insurance coverage through an employer. Individuals who receive health insurance coverage through an employer often have the advantages of group rates, risk pooling, and cost sharing that are not available to individuals who purchase health insurance on their own. One distinct advantage to employer-provided health insurance is the Federal, and sometimes state, tax advantages that accrue to employees. The value of employer-sponsored health insurance is excludable from an employee's income for Federal income tax and employment tax purposes, which has the effect of reducing the net cost of health insurance for the employee. In addition, there are other Federal tax advantages, such as the benefits for cafeteria plans, flexible spending arrangements, and health savings arrangements that increase the incentives for employees to prefer to receive health insurance through an employer.

On the other hand, employers generally are indifferent from a Federal tax perspective about whether to pay compensation in cash or in the form of health insurance. This is because the employer is entitled to deduct the costs of health insurance in the same way that the employer deducts other compensation costs. Thus, there is no specific Federal tax advantage to the employer to providing health insurance to employees.

Chapter 2 - Many small employers do not offer health insurance. The Small Employer Health Insurance Tax Credit was established to help eligible small employers—businesses or tax-exempt entities—provide health insurance for employees. The base of the credit is premiums paid or the average premium for an employer's state if premiums paid were higher. In 2010, for small businesses, the credit was 35 percent of the base unless the business had more than 10 FTE employees or paid average annual wages over $25,000.

GAO was asked to examine (1) the extent to which the credit is claimed and any factors that limit claims, including how they can be addressed; (2) how fully IRS is ensuring that the credit is correctly claimed; and (3) what data are needed to evaluate the effects of the credit.

GAO compared IRS data on credit claims with estimates of eligible employers, interviewed various credit stakeholders and IRS officials as well as academicians on evaluation, compared IRS credit compliance documents with the rules and practices used for prior tax provisions and IRS strategic objectives, and reviewed literature and data.

In: Small Business Health Insurance   ISBN: 978-1-62417-239-7
Editor: Ibrahim N. McCormick   © 2013 Nova Science Publishers, Inc.

Chapter 1

HEALTH INSURANCE IN THE SMALL BUSINESS MARKET: AVAILABILITY, COVERAGE, AND THE EFFECT OF TAX INCENTIVES*

Quantria Strategies LLC

EXECUTIVE SUMMARY

Sources of Health Insurance Coverage

In the United States, most people get health insurance either through their employer or through a spouse's or parent's employer. According to the most recent estimates of the Current Population Survey (CPS), March 2010 Supplement, 55.8 percent of the U.S. population have access to health insurance through an employer, 30.6 percent have access to health insurance through a government program (such as Medicare, Medicaid, or SCHIP), 8.9 percent privately purchase health insurance on their own, and 16.7 percent are uninsured.

---

* This is an edited, reformatted and augmented version of the Small Business Administration, Office of Advocacy, SBAHQ-09-Q-0018, dated September 2011.

Historically, there have been distinct advantages to obtaining health insurance coverage through an employer. Individuals who receive health insurance coverage through an employer often have the advantages of group rates, risk pooling, and cost sharing that are not available to individuals who purchase health insurance on their own. One distinct advantage to employer-provided health insurance is the Federal, and sometimes state, tax advantages that accrue to employees. The value of employer-sponsored health insurance is excludable from an employee's income for Federal income tax and employment tax purposes, which has the effect of reducing the net cost of health insurance for the employee. In addition, there are other Federal tax advantages, such as the benefits for cafeteria plans, flexible spending arrangements, and health savings arrangements that increase the incentives for employees to prefer to receive health insurance through an employer.

On the other hand, employers generally are indifferent from a Federal tax perspective about whether to pay compensation in cash or in the form of health insurance. This is because the employer is entitled to deduct the costs of health insurance in the same way that the employer deducts other compensation costs. Thus, there is no specific Federal tax advantage to the employer to providing health insurance to employees.[1]

Small Businesses and Health Insurance Coverage[2]

Access to employer-sponsored health insurance correlates positively with business size. The smallest businesses are the least likely and the largest businesses are the most likely to make health insurance available to their employees. In 2009, 55 percent of U.S. private sector establishments offered health insurance to their employees. For firms with 100-999 employees, 94.3 percent of establishments offered health insurance to their employees and for firms with 1,000 or more employees, 99.2 percent of establishments offered health insurance to their employees. By contrast, for firms with fewer than 10 employees, only 33.1 percent of establishments offered health insurance to employees and for firms with 10 to 24 employees, the establishment access rate was 62.5 percent. Access rates are even lower for establishments with predominantly low wage employees, with access rates as low as 17.9 percent of establishments (for firms with fewer than 10 employees).

On the other hand, when employers offer health insurance, employees tend to accept the coverage at about the same rate, irrespective of the size of the business – referred to as the take-up rate. In March 2010, the health insurance take-up rate was 71 percent by employees at firms with 1 to 49 employees, 73 percent by employees at firms with 50 to 99 employees, 74 percent by employees at firms with 100 to 499 employees, and 79 percent by employees at firms with 500 or more employees.

Many small businesses organize as sole proprietorships, partnerships, and S corporations; for Federal tax purposes; this means that these types of businesses are not subject to the Federal corporate income tax, but instead are subject to tax on the individual income tax returns of the business owners. The owner of a corporation who works for the corporation is treated as an employee for Federal tax purposes and the corporation can deduct the costs of health insurance purchased for the owner. However, the owner of a sole proprietorship, partnership, or S corporation generally is not treated as an employee under the Federal tax laws. As a result, the deduction for employer contributions to a health plan does not apply to these so-called self-employed individuals. Instead, they are entitled to claim the self-employed health insurance deduction. This self-employed health insurance deduction is only allowed for income tax purposes; it is not allowed for employment tax purposes.[3]

Many small businesses in the United States do not have any employees other than the business owner. In 2008, there were 21.4 million small businesses without employees in the United States.[4] Unless they have health insurance coverage available through other employment or through a spouse's employment, these self-employed individuals must obtain their health insurance coverage in the individual insurance market.

In 2008, 17 percent of Federal income tax returns reporting no income from self-employment also reported the self-employed health insurance deduction. The use of the self-employed health insurance deduction correlates positively with income – the likelihood of claiming the deduction increases with income. In 2008, 84 percent of self-employed returns with adjusted gross income of $500,000 or more claimed the self-employed health insurance deduction, whereas only 9 percent of self-employed returns with adjusted gross income between $10,000 and $20,000 claimed the deduction.[5]

Access to health insurance coverage among employees of small businesses is one of the most intractable problems facing the U.S. health care system. Small businesses face a variety of barriers to offering health insurance coverage to their employees. The costs of health insurance are typically much higher for employees of small businesses. In addition, small businesses face significantly higher administrative costs per employee to offer health insurance and their overall costs are less predictable than the costs of large businesses. Employees of small businesses tend to receive lower wages compared to employees of large businesses, making low-wage employees less likely to prefer health insurance benefits to higher wages.

Effects of the Recession on the Availability of Employer Health Insurance

The recession that began in December 2007 adversely affected access to employer health insurance. A recent Employee Benefits Research Institute study found that employer-based health insurance coverage declined by 4.3 percent between September of 2007 and April of 2009. The largest decline in coverage occurred among employees of firms with less than 25 employees (10.7 percent decline). The decline among employees of firms with 100 or more employees was 3.5 percent.

However, employer access rates for health insurance have generally declined over time among small business employers. For firms with fewer than 10 employees, establishment access rates have declined from a high of 39.3 percent in 1999 to 33.6 percent in 2009. For firms with 10 to 24 employees, establishment access rates have declined from 69.9 percent (1999) to 62.5 percent (2009). For firms with 25 to 99 employees, establishment access rates have declined from 85.3 percent (1999) to 81.6 percent (2009). For firms with 100 to 499 employees, establishment access rates have shown less volatility, fluctuating between 93 percent to slightly less than 95 percent.

Geographic Difference in Health Insurance Offer Rates

Employer health insurance access rates also vary geographically. Offer rates tend to be higher in the Northeast and lower in the Southwest. These differences are likely to reflect a variety of factors, including: (1) employers in geographic areas compete for the same employees and, therefore, are likely to offer similar benefit packages and (2) there may be higher concentrations of employers that are less likely to offer health insurance in certain geographic areas, such as those areas that are less urban.

One question is whether the geographic disparities in health insurance access rates might be attributable to state mandates and/or state tax incentives designed to require or encourage employers to offer health insurance to their employees. For example, in Hawaii, an employer mandate requires employers to offer health insurance and the access rates reflect this state law requirement.

Eleven states have adopted special tax incentives designed to encourage small businesses to offer health insurance to their employees. However, in most cases, these tax incentives apply to a very narrow class of small businesses (typically the smallest businesses) or are relatively narrow incentives. There is no evidence that any of the tax incentives adopted at the state level have had any positive effect on employer health insurance access rates.

Federal Tax Incentives

Given the size of Federal tax benefits relative to the tax incentives offered by the states, it is relevant to examine what effect the Federal tax benefits might have on employer health insurance. We estimate that small corporations (those with less than $10 million in assets) claimed deductions for employer health insurance of $18.8 billion in 2007 (the most recent data available). In 2007, self-employed taxpayers claimed $21.2 billion for the self-employed health insurance deduction; the average amount claimed per return was $5,544. Approximately half of the tax benefits of the self-employed health insurance deduction accrue to taxpayers with adjusted gross income of at least $100,000.

The exclusion from employee income for employer health insurance cost approximately $246 billion in 2007, according to estimates of the Joint Committee on Taxation. This tax savings included income taxes ($145.3 billion) and payroll taxes ($100.7 billion).

Small Business Health Insurance Tax Credit

The Patient Protection and Affordable Care Act of 2010 (hereinafter "Health Care Reform Act") adopted comprehensive changes to the U.S. health insurance system. In 2014, the Act will set up state health exchanges that will offer individuals and small businesses access to health insurance, provide greater regulation of health insurance, and provide tax credits for individuals and small businesses to help offset the cost of health insurance.

The Health Care Reform Act affects small businesses in a variety of ways. Small businesses with 50 or more employees are assessed a $2,000 per worker fee if they do not provide health insurance to their employees and if any of their employees receive subsidized health insurance coverage through a health insurance exchange. Beginning in 2014, small businesses with less than 100 employees will have access to health insurance through the state exchanges and, starting in 2017, the states will have the option of expanding the states' exchanges to businesses with more than 100 employees.

One of the most significant aspects of health care reform for small businesses is the adoption of a generous tax credit to help subsidize the cost of small business health insurance. The credit is nonrefundable and is available only to offset current Federal income tax.[6] Thus, employers who do not have sufficient current Federal income tax and Medicare tax liability cannot fully utilize the credit; employers may carry back one year and carry forward 20 years the unused credits.

A recent analysis by the Lewin Group for Families USA and Small Business Majority estimated that approximately 4 million small businesses will be eligible for the small business health insurance tax credit nationwide and that approximately 1.2 million of these businesses will be eligible for the full small business health insurance tax credit. It is important to distinguish between eligibility for the credit and ability to apply the credit to current tax liabilities. Eligibility means that by virtue of the firm characteristics, the small business is eligible to claim the credit. Because the credit is nonrefundable, an employer can only use the credit if the employer has positive Federal tax liability that the credit can offset.

Conclusions

Individuals who lack health insurance coverage in the United States are more likely to work for a small employer compared to a large employer. The participation rates (access rate multiplied by take-up rate) in employer-provided health insurance are shown in the following table. The table shows that the participation rate in employer-provided health insurance correlates positively with employer size.

Table 1. Access, Take-Up, and Participation Rates, by Establishment Size (Numbers are Percentages)

Establishment Size, by Employment	Access	Take-up Rates	Participation
1 to 49	55	70	39
50 to 99	70	72	50
100 to 499	82	72	59
500 or more	88	78	68
Total All Firms	71	73	51

Source: U.S. Bureau of Labor Statistics, National Compensation Survey, March 2010.

States have tried a variety of approaches to improve health insurance coverage and, particularly, to improve the offering of health insurance by small businesses. However, we found that most existing state-tax incentive programs apply to very narrow classes of employers (typically the smallest of employers) and provide relatively narrow tax benefits. We found no correlation between any of these tax incentives and employee access rates for health insurance.

The new Federal tax credit for small employer health insurance, effective beginning in 2010, offers a more generous incentive to encourage small businesses to offer health insurance to their employees. However, because the credit is nonrefundable, many employers will not be able to take full advantage of it. In addition, the credit is most likely to benefit those small businesses that currently offer health insurance to their employees. Other small businesses are likely to wait to see how Federal healthcare reform affects overall health care costs in the United States before adopting a plan to offer health insurance to their employees.

I. INTRODUCTION

Since the 1940's, most Americans have obtained their health insurance coverage through employer-sponsored health insurance. Employer-sponsored health insurance offers distinct advantages over private purchases of health insurance, including favorable tax treatment for Federal tax purposes and, in many cases, state income tax.

In addition to the favorable tax treatment, individuals who have access to health insurance through an employer typically have the advantages of scale economies and risk distribution that make employer-sponsored health insurance significantly cheaper than comparable privately purchased health insurance coverage. However, these advantages disappear for small employers who face high per employee costs to offer health insurance. The smaller the employer, the more likely the per-employee costs will be similar to the costs of privately purchased health insurance.[7] Further, the high administrative costs that small employers face to offer health insurance coverage to employees often drives small employers out of this market.

A goal of the favorable tax treatment of employer-sponsored health insurance was to lead employees to prefer health insurance coverage in lieu of cash wages. However, the Federal tax system does not provide a specific tax advantage to employers to encourage them to provide employer-sponsored health insurance instead of wages or other benefits and, the smaller the employer, the more likely that the costs of employer-sponsored health insurance creates a deterrent to providing this coverage. In addition, the specific demographics of small business employees make them more likely to prefer cash wages to benefits.

As a result, employee access to health insurance correlates positively with firm size. In 2009, 33.6 percent of establishments with fewer than 10 employees offered employer-sponsored health insurance, while nearly 100 percent of establishments of firms with 1,000 or more employees offered health insurance to their employees.[8]

The lack of access to affordable health insurance for employees of small businesses has been one of the most intractable problems facing the U.S. health care system. States have experimented with a variety of approaches to address this problem, including the adoption of specific reforms to make is easier for small businesses to obtain affordable health insurance for their employees and, in some limited cases, state tax incentives to encourage small employers to offer employer-sponsored health insurance to their employees.

Federal health care reform enacted in 2010 will have wide-ranging impacts on the availability of health insurance in the United States. However, because this legislation does not require employers to offer health insurance to their employees, the issues about access to employer-sponsored health insurance will remain important. Federal health care reform should make it easier for small businesses to offer health insurance to their employees because reform will permit small businesses to participate in the health insurance exchanges at the state level. In addition, the reform legislation adopts a small business health insurance tax credit to help small businesses offset the costs of employer-sponsored health insurance for their employees.

This paper offers an overview of the issues and status of small business health insurance in the United States. Utilizing data from the Medical Expenditure Panel Survey (MEPS), the Current Population Survey (CPS), the Survey of Income and Program Participation (SIPP), the Kaiser Family Foundation Annual Survey of Employer Health Benefits, and tax return data from the Internal Revenue Service, the paper examines trends in access to employer-sponsored health insurance by small businesses.

This paper also specifically examines the question of whether existing tax incentives at the Federal and state level provide sufficient inducement to small businesses to adopt health insurance plans for their employees. Using data from the MEPS that allows a look at establishment health insurance access rates by firm size on a state-by-state basis, the paper examines employer tax incentives adopted by Kansas and Montana to examine whether the tax incentives have had a measurable effect on the rate at which small businesses offer health insurance to their employees in these states. We found that state tax incentives have generally not led to measurable increases in the percentage of small businesses offering health insurance to employees, primarily because the level of the tax incentives provided have been relatively small.

In addition, we examine the small business health insurance tax credit adopted as part of the Federal health care reform legislation. Based on our research of the firms eligible for this credit and IRS Statistics of Income (SOI) data, we estimate the number of small businesses that may be able to benefit from the small business tax credit.

II. HEALTH INSURANCE COVERAGE AND EMPLOYMENT-BASED HEALTH INSURANCE IN THE UNITED STATES

A. Sources of Health Insurance Coverage

Historically, the predominant source of health insurance coverage in the United States has been employer-provided health insurance. Employers began offering health insurance as an employee benefit during the 1940's, when wage controls limited pay and employers sought to compete for scarce workers.[9] In 1943, the National War Labor Board ruled that employer contributions to insurance did not count as wages and employers could offer insurance in addition to wages and salaries.[10] Because of this ruling, employers began offering health insurance to circumvent wage controls and compete for workers in the labor market, marking the beginning of the trend toward employment-based health insurance coverage for workers. By negotiating benefits on behalf of broad groups of workers, unions also contributed to the trend toward employment-based health insurance.

According to the 2010 Current Population Survey (CPS) March Supplement, 55.8 percent of the U.S. population (approximately 170 million people) had employment-based health insurance, 30.6 percent (approximately 93 million people) utilized such government health insurance programs as Medicare, Medicaid, military health care, and SCHIP; 8.9 percent (approximately 27 million people) purchased individual health insurance plans; and 16.7 percent (approximately 51 million people) were uninsured.[11] Graph 1 shows this breakdown of sources of health insurance.[12]

The sources of health insurance coverage vary somewhat from year-to-year. However, 2009 marked the first year since 1987 that the number of people with health insurance declined. The percent of individuals who were uninsured increased significantly from 2008 to 2009 (15.4 compared to 16.7, respectively). In addition, for those individuals with insurance coverage, the composition of coverage also changed.[13] For instance, the availability of employment-based health insurance declined in 2009 (55.8 percent in 2009 compared to 58.5 percent in 2008). Coverage by a government health insurance plan increased from 29.0 to 30.6 percent from 2008 to 2009. Purchases of individually purchased health insurance remained unchanged at approximately 8.9 percent.[14]

Over time, the cost of health insurance has increased significantly. The growing cost of providing employer-sponsored health insurance increases total compensation costs for employers. Since the 1960's, employment-based health insurance has become a larger and larger share of total compensation costs. For example, U.S. employers spent $25 billion on health insurance in 1960 (expressed in 2008 dollars). This figure grew to $545 billion in 2008.[15] Thus, in constant dollar terms, employer health insurance costs grew twenty-two fold during this period. Graph 2 displays the averages by decade for the total amount that U.S. employers spent on health insurance. As shown in Graph 2, the cost of this health insurance coverage increased significantly with each period.

Further, employer health insurance costs have become a larger percentage of total compensation costs.[16] Graph 3 shows health insurance and non-health employee benefits as a percentage of total compensation since the 1960's. Health insurance benefits were 1.4 percent of total compensation during the 1960's and increased to 6.6 percent in 2008.[17] On the other hand, the costs for non-health related benefits rose from 7.7 percent in the 1960's to 13.0 percent in the 1980's and have declined to 11.8 percent in the 2000's.[18]

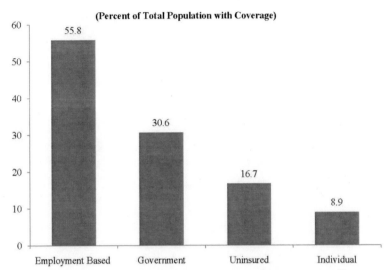

Source: 2010 Current Population Survey, March 2010 Supplement.

Graph 1. Sources of Health Insurance Coverage in the United States, 2009.

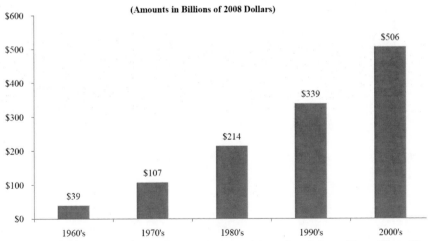

Source: *Snapshots: Health Care Costs. Wages and Benefits: A Long-Term View.* The Kaiser Family Foundation, November 2009.

Graph 2. Employer Costs for Private Group Health Benefits in the United States, Average Costs for selected Decades.

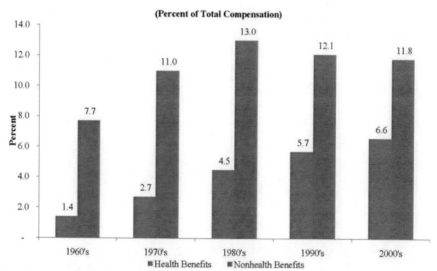

Source: *Snapshots: Health Care Costs. Wages and Benefits: A Long-Term View.* The Kaiser Family Foundation, November 2009.

Graph 3. Average Health and Nonhealth Benefits as a Share of Total Compensation in the United States, Selected Time Periods 1960's to 2000's.

The costs of employment-based health insurance have also increased as a percentage of GDP during the same periods. While total compensation costs have remained stable over time, ranging from 56 to 59 percent of GDP, employer health care costs have increased from 0.6 percent of GDP in 1960 to 3.8 percent in 2008.[19]

B. Advantages of Employer-Provided Health Insurance

1. Employer-Provided Health Insurance is a Compensation Cost for Employers

Much has been written about the so-called "favorable tax status" of employer-provided health insurance and many have opined that this favorable tax status has led to the burgeoning costs of employment-based health insurance as well as encouraging employers to offer more comprehensive coverage than they would otherwise provide. On the other hand, a 2008 report by the Congressional Research Service stated that "the historical argument about the importance of tax regulatory policies [in the increases in employer-sponsored health insurance] may be overstated."[20]

It is important to understand the differences between the tax benefits to employers and the tax benefits to employees of employment-based health insurance. Employers are entitled to deduct the costs of their contributions to employment-based health insurance. However, these costs represent compensation costs that would otherwise be deductible if, instead of providing health insurance, the employer paid the same amount directly to employees.[21] Thus, from a Federal tax perspective, employers are neutral as to the decision to provide cash wages to employees or to provide employees with an equivalent amount in benefits such as health insurance.[22]

Employers compete for workers by offering wage and benefit packages that will attract and retain employees. Employers offer noncash benefits like health insurance to their employees in lieu of cash wages because employees value these benefits more than they value cash wages. This can occur for two primary reasons. First, the amounts that an employer pays for health insurance coverage on behalf of employees are not currently included in employees' income for Federal (and sometimes state) income tax purposes and for employment tax purposes. Thus, a dollar of health insurance coverage is worth more to an employee than a dollar of wages. Second, employers purchasing health insurance may be able to negotiate better rates so that the cost of health insurance coverage for an employee is lower if purchased through an employer than it would be if the employee purchased the coverage directly.

An important point to consider is that, for employees, there is a direct tradeoff between cash wages and employer-provided health insurance. When employers pay for health insurance for their employees, economists generally believe that the employer's costs for health insurance translate to lower wages for workers. Thus, employees receive less in current wages because of the amounts their employers pay for health insurance.[23] Further, if an employee elects to receive employer-provided health insurance, the employee has lower wages for employment tax purposes. While this has the effect of reducing the amount of employment taxes the employee pays, it also may reduce the amount of Social Security benefits to which the employee may be entitled when he or she retires.

The costs of health insurance for an employer include the direct costs of the insurance coverage itself as well as the indirect costs of offering this benefit in lieu of current wages. For example, an employer has administrative costs related to processing employee elections with respect to health insurance coverage as well as the costs of researching and securing a health insurance provider (or providers).

2. Tax Advantages Create Incentives for Employees to Prefer Employer-Provided Health Insurance

Employees, on the other hand, do have specific tax advantages that lead them to prefer to receive health insurance (and other tax-favored benefits, such as retirement savings) to cash compensation. From an employee's perspective, there are Federal tax advantages and sometimes, state tax advantages to employer-provided health insurance.

Federal tax advantages

From a Federal tax perspective, several tax benefits accrue from employer-provided health insurance. First, the value of the employer's contribution to health insurance is excludable from the employee's income for income tax and employment tax purposes.[24] The value of any benefits the employee receives under the health insurance policy also is excluded from income.

In addition, in some cases, the employee's share of the costs of health insurance coverage may be excluded from income. For example, employers can set up plans (cafeteria plans, flexible spending arrangements, and Health Savings Accounts (HSAs)) that allow employees to pay for out-of-pocket medical expenses on a pre-tax basis. Overall, the Federal tax system provides strong incentives for employees to prefer to receive health insurance through an employer.

Because the Federal income tax is a progressive tax system in which the tax rates increase as total income increases, the greater an employee's income, the greater the value an employee receives for the exclusion from income for employer-provided health insurance. Thus, an employee in a 15 percent Federal income tax bracket receives a smaller dollar benefit from the exclusion for employer-provided health insurance than an employee in the 25 percent Federal income tax bracket.

Federal employment taxes for social security and disability income (OASDI) and for hospital insurance under Medicare (HI) apply at a rate of 15.3 percent of compensation. OASDI taxes apply at a rate of 12.4 percent up to the taxable wage base ($106,800 for 2010); the employee and employer each pay half of these taxes. The HI tax rate is 2.9 percent of all compensation, which the employee and the employer also split equally. Thus, in the case of Federal employment taxes, the value of the exclusion for employer-provided health insurance is equal to 15.3 percent of compensation up to the taxable wage base and then 2.9 percent of compensation thereafter. Economists generally believe that employees ultimately bear the burden of the employer's share of Federal employment taxes.[25] Thus, the employees theoretically accrue the advantage of the exclusion for the employer share of employment taxes.

Table 2 shows examples of the value of the Federal tax benefits for three sets of employees. The examples show the effects on a single individual of receiving $5,000 of health insurance from an employer and the alternative effect if the individual receives an additional $5,000 in cash compensation.

Table 2. Examples of the Value of Federal Tax Benefits to Employees for Employer-Provided Health Insurance (2009 Federal Tax Rates)

	Employee A		Employee B		Employee C	
	$25,000 compensation; no employer-provided health insurance	$20,000 compensation; $5,000 of employer-provided health insurance	$50,000 compensation; no employer-provided health insurance	$45,000 compensation; $5,000 of employer-provided health insurance	$100,000 compensation; no employer-provided health insurance	$95,000 compensation; $5,000 of employer-provided health insurance
1. Taxable income, all from compensation with employer	$15,650	$10,650	$40,650	$35,650	$90,650	$85,650
2. Total Federal income taxes	$1,934	$1,184	$6,356	$5,106	$19,109	$17,709
3. Total Federal OASDHI taxes (15.3% of cash compensation)	$3,825	$3,060	$7,650	$6,885	$15,300	$14,535
4. Value of Federal income tax exclusion (difference between income tax with all cash compensation and income tax with $5,000 of health insurance)	$0	$750	$0	$1,250	$0	$1,400
5. Value of Federal employment tax exclusion (15.3% of excluded compensation)	$0	$765	$0	$765	$0	$765
6. Total Federal tax savings from employer-provided health insurance (sum of 4. and 5.)	$0	$1,515	$0	$2,015	$0	$2,165

Source: Authors' calculations using 2009 Federal tax rate schedules. In order to isolate the effect of the exclusion for employer-provided health insurance, this example assumes a single individual claiming one personal exemption, the standard deduction, and no other income, exclusions, deductions, or credits. In addition, the example ignores the possible effects of the individual medical expense deduction.

For Employee A, the $5,000 worth of health insurance has a net cost, after Federal tax savings, of $3,485 ($5,000 minus $1,515 of savings); this represents a net cost of 70 percent of the pre-tax cost. For Employee B, the net cost of $5,000 worth of employer-provided health insurance is $2,985 ($5,000 minus $2,015); this represents 60 percent of the pre-tax cost. For Employee C, the net cost is $2,835 ($5,000 minus $2,165); this represents 57 percent of the pre-tax cost. As employee income rises, the net cost of $5,000 declines. Thus, the examples show that the value of the income tax exclusion increases as an employee's marginal income tax rate increases, making it more valuable to employees in higher income tax brackets. Further, the value of the employment tax exclusion is equivalent in all of these examples because none of the employees earn more than the social security taxable wage base (which was $106,800 for 2009). As employees' compensation exceeds the taxable wage base, the value of the employment tax exclusion declines.

State tax advantages

In addition to the Federal tax advantages, there may also be tax advantages accruing to employees at the state level from the receipt of health insurance through an employer. In states with income tax systems, the Federal exclusion generally applies for state income tax purposes so that the amounts excluded from income for Federal income tax purposes also receive the state income tax exclusion. The value of the exclusion will depend upon the tax rate structure in effect in the state. In those states without an income tax, the exclusion from income is irrelevant.

3. Nontax Advantages Create Additional Incentives

In addition to the tax advantages that accrue to employees who receive health insurance through an employer, powerful nontax advantages can drive demand for employer-sponsored health insurance. These nontax benefits accrue to both employers and employees.

Healthy employees

For employers, a healthy workforce can reduce workdays lost to sickness. There is a general belief that people who have health insurance tend to be healthier than those people who do not have health insurance. However, there is a "chicken and egg" problem with this analysis because individuals who have health insurance tend to have a more stable relationship with the workforce, have higher income, and have more education than those without health insurance.[26] All of these factors could contribute separately to the overall better health of those individuals with health insurance.

Group rates/negotiating power

Employers have more bargaining power than individuals have and can negotiate better rates for health insurance than individual employees could negotiate on their own. Particularly with respect to large employers, the economies of scale afforded by group health insurance offer significant savings in the cost of health insurance relative to purchases in the individual market. Thus, the operation of the marketplace for group health insurance provides a powerful incentive to prefer health insurance through an employer.

This may not be intuitively obvious since many surveys show health insurance premiums in the nongroup market are similar to (or even lower than) those in the employer group health market. However, statistics that look only at premiums fail to account for differences in the type of health insurance coverage provided. In addition, people who are purchasing health insurance in the nongroup market are, on average, healthier than people who have employer-sponsored health insurance.[27] Despite the difference in the demographics of the nongroup group market compared the employer-sponsored health insurance market, individuals purchasing nongroup health insurance pay a higher proportion (52 percent) of their health expenditures out of pocket compared to those with employer-sponsored health insurance (30 percent out of pocket), suggesting that nongroup health insurance provides less coverage than employer-sponsored health insurance.[28]

Cost sharing

If employers pay part of the cost of their employees' health insurance coverage, employees may perceive that they are receiving more in compensation than their cash wages. Although economists believe that employees ultimately bear the full burden of these costs that are "shared" by an employer, employee perception may not conform to this theory.

Risk pool advantages

A fundamental theory of insurance is the spreading of risks across a group. Risk pooling works because, when a large number of people are included in the pool covering the costs of their health care, the larger the group, the more stable the average costs become. This is because the high costs of any one individual have a smaller effect on the average as the group gets bigger.

Employment-based health insurance can be advantageous because of risk pooling. For large employers, the size of their group receiving health insurance coverage is large enough for the benefits of risk pooling to occur.

III. HEALTH INSURANCE IN THE SMALL BUSINESS MARKET

A. Access to Health Insurance Coverage in the Small Business Sector

1. Small Business Health Insurance Access Rate by Employer Size

As noted above, approximately 60 percent of workers in U.S. establishments receive health insurance through an employer. In 2009, 55 percent of private sector establishments offered health insurance to their employees.[29] However, the percentage of private-sector establishments offering health insurance to their employees is directly correlated to firm size; as the size of the firm grows, so does the percentage of firms offering health insurance to employees. Table 3 shows the percentage of firms offering health insurance by firm size for 2009 and by other firm characteristics.

As Table 3 shows, small firms and firms with predominantly low-wage workers are significantly less likely to offer health insurance to employees. While 99.2 percent of establishments for firms with 1,000 or more employees offered health insurance to their employees in 2009, the establishment access rate was only 33.6 percent for firms with fewer than 10 employees. Unincorporated firms, many of which are likely to be doing business as sole proprietorships, are less likely to be offering health insurance than firms of the same size category that are incorporated.[30] The likelihood of offering health insurance to employees also varies across industries, as shown in Table 4, below.

Table 4 shows that the agriculture, fishing, and forestry industry (26.4 percent), construction (42.3 percent), other services (45.4 percent), and utilities and transportation (57.1 percent) have lower access rates for health insurance than other industries, which range from an access rate of 59.1 percent (retail trade) to 67.8 percent (financial services and real estate). Even by industry, however, the establishment access rate is considerably lower for the smallest firms than for the largest firms.

Table 3. Percentage of Private Sector Establishments Offering Health Insurance to Employees, 2009, by firm size and other selected characteristics

Firm Size, by employment	Total	>50% Low Wage Employees*	<50% Low Wage Employees	Incorporated (for profit)	Unincorporated (for profit)
All Firms	55.0	41.0	62.2	59.6	37.9
Fewer than 10	33.6	17.9	41.7	36.3	25.5
10-24	62.5	32.8	76.4	65.1	49.5
25-99	81.6	59.5	91.4	81.8	72.8
100-999	94.3	88.7	97.1	93.4	92.5
1000 or more	99.2	98.5	99.7	99.3	99.0

Source: Agency for Healthcare Research and Quality, Center for Financing, Access and Cost Trends, 2009 Medical Expenditure Panel Survey – Insurance Component (MEPS-IC), Table I.A.2. The MEPS-IC data are collected at the establishment level. However, for purposes of identifying the appropriate size classification for establishments, firm level data are used.

* Low Wage Employees are defined as employees earning at or below the 25th percentile for all hourly wages in the United States. For 2009, a Low Wage Employee is one who earns no more than $11.00 per hour.

Table 4. Percentage of Private Sector Establishments Offering Health Insurance to Employees, 2009 by firm size and industry group

Industry Group	All Firms	Less than 10 Employees	10-24 Employees	25-99 Employees	100-999 Employees	1,000 or More Employees
Agriculture, fishing, forestry	26.4	20.6	39.1	83.1	68.2	100.0
Mining and manufacturing	67.7	43.0	79.2	90.4	97.9	99.8
Construction	42.3	31.1	73.5	87.8	87,8	100.0
Utilities and transportation	57.1	26.7	67.8	84.5	94.2	99.3
Wholesale trade	66.6	44.9	81.8	90.2	98.5	99.0
Financial services and real estate	67.8	39.0	75.7	90.0	97.4	98.5
Retail trade	59.1	25.5	60.4	84.7	93.0	99.6
Professional services	58.8	40.7	72.3	88.1	97.8	99.4
Other services	45.4	28.1	43.4	65.2	86.1	99.4

Source: Agency for Healthcare Research and Quality, Center for Financial, Access and Cost Trends, 2009 Medical Expenditure Panel Survey – Insurance Component, Table I.A.2.

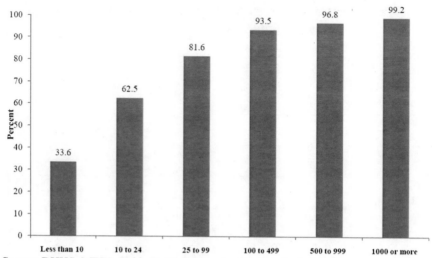

Source: DHHS, MEPS, Table II A2, 2009and author's calculations.

Graph 4. Percent of Private-Sector U.S. Establishments that Offer Health Insurance, Firm Size by Employment, 2009.

Graph 4 displays the percent of private sector establishments that offer health insurance to their employees. The largest firms, those with 500 or more employees have offer rates approaching 100 percent. The smallest firms, on the other hand, have an offer rate of 33.6 percent. Graph 4 shows that the likelihood of an employer offering health insurance increases steadily with firm size.

2. Take-Up Rates

Workplace Coverage

How many individuals actually have employer provided health insurance coverage depends upon both the offer rate and the take-up rate. Offer rates indicate whether or not an employee has access to health insurance in the workplace. However, access tells only part of the story. Assuming an employee has access to health insurance coverage at work, the decision to accept the employer-provided health insurance (take-up rate) affects the numbers of workers covered by the plan. The participation rate is the product of the offer and take-up rates.

The Bureau of Labor Statistics (BLS) provides estimates of access (offer rates) and take-up rates of employer-sponsored health insurance by establishment size.[31] Table 5 displays the BLS access and take-up rates from the March 2010 National Compensation Survey (NCS). Take-up rates tend to show less variation by establishment size. Approximately 70-80 percent of employees who are offered health insurance through an employer take up or accept the insurance.

Table 5 shows that participation rates, which equal access rates multiplied by take-up rates, correlate positively with firm size. Thus, while 70 to 72 percent of small business employees take advantage of employer-sponsored health insurance that is offered, the rate of establishment offering means that participation rates are significantly lower for these employees. For the smallest establishments (those with less than 50 employees), only 39 percent of employees participate in employer-sponsored health insurance.

A recent study by the Employee Benefits Research Institute (EBRI) indicates that participation rates have remained stable since the late 1980s.[32] EBRI reports that in most cases, employees who decline workplace health insurance coverage are more likely to have coverage from another employer or from a spouse. Further, EBRI estimated that less than 4 percent of workers eligible for workplace health insurance coverage remained uninsured between 1995 and 2005.[33]

Self-Employed Coverage

Many small businesses are organized as sole proprietorships, partnerships, and S corporations. For Federal income tax purposes, these types of businesses are not subject to the corporate income tax. Instead, the owners of the businesses are subject to tax on business income on their individual income tax returns. This distinction has important implications for the treatment of health insurance. The owner of a corporation who works for the corporation is treated as an employee, i.e., a wage and salary worker, for Federal tax purposes. Thus, the cost of health insurance for the owner of a corporation is deductible for income and employment tax purposes. However, the owner of a sole proprietorship, partnership, or S corporation generally is not treated as an employee, but is treated as a self-employed individual. The deduction for employer contributions to a health plan does not apply to these self-employed individuals. Instead, they are entitled to claim the self-employed health insurance deduction. The self-employed health insurance deduction is only allowed for income tax purposes; it is not allowed for employment tax purposes.[34]

Many small businesses in the United States do not have any employees other than the business owner. In 2008, there were 21.4 million small businesses without employees in the United States.[35] Unless they have health insurance coverage available through other employment or through a spouse's employment, these self-employed individuals must obtain their health insurance coverage in the privately purchased individual insurance market.

Table 5. Access, Take-Up, and Participation Rates, by Establishment Size (Percent)

Establishment Size, by Employment	Access	Take-up	Participation
1 to 49	55	70	39
50 to 99	70	72	50
100 to 499	82	72	59
500 or more	88	78	68
Total All Firms	71	73	51

Source: BLS, National Compensation Survey, Employee Benefits in the United States, March 2010.

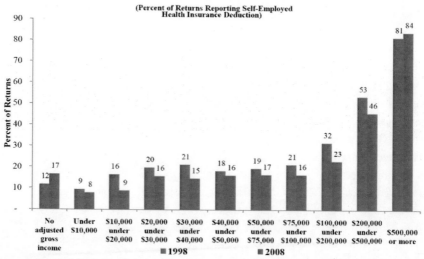

Source: Internal Revenue Service, Statistics of Income, Individual Income Tax Return Data, Tax Years 1998 and 2008.

Graph 5. Percent of Returns with Self-Employment Income Claiming the Self-Employed Health Insurance Deduction Tax Years 1998 and 2008, Distributed by AGI.

Graph 5 displays the use of the self-employed health insurance deduction for 1998 and 2008, showing that the use of the deduction correlates positively with income. Overall in 2008, only 17 percent of returns reporting no self-employment income also reported the deduction for self-employed health insurance.

Closer inspection indicates that over the 1998 to 2008 period, the percent of returns with self-employed income that reported the deduction for self-employed health insurance declined for all but two income classes (Graph 5). Returns with adjusted gross incomes of $500,000 or more (less than one-tenth of one percent of all returns reporting self-employed business income) as well as those returns with no net income (3 percent of all returns reporting self-employed business income) reported an increase in the deduction for self-employed health insurance coverage.[36]

3. Cost and Quality of Health Insurance

The data show that at least 70 percent of individuals who have access to health insurance through an employer-sponsored health plan participate in such insurance, irrespective of firm size. However, the type of health insurance coverage to which employees have access can also vary by firm size. While the idea of the quality of health insurance coverage can be subjective and, therefore, difficult to quantify, there is some evidence that the health insurance offered to employees of small firms differs from the health insurance offered to employees of large firms. A 2003 Small Business Administration study used the actuarial value of a health plan as a measure of the plan's generosity; the actuarial value measures how much of the health expenditures of a standard employed population are paid by the health plan.[37] This study found that the actuarial value of a health insurance plan for firms with fewer than 10 employees average 78 percent of expected costs, while the actuarial value of health insurance plans for firms with 1,000 or more employees was 83 percent of expected costs.

In general, employer-sponsored health insurance premiums are higher for employees of small firms than for employees of large firms. Graph 6 shows the average total single premium per enrolled employee by firm size for 2009. While the average premium across all firms is $4,669, the average for firms with fewer than 10 employees is $4,982 and the average for firms with 1,000 or more employees is $4,673. Interestingly, the average single premiums for firms with 10 to 24 employees and for firms with 25 to 99 employees are lower than the average for firms with 1,000 or more employees, but this may reflect differences in other plan characteristics, such as deductibles and copayments. Graph 7 provides the average total family premium by firm size for 2009.

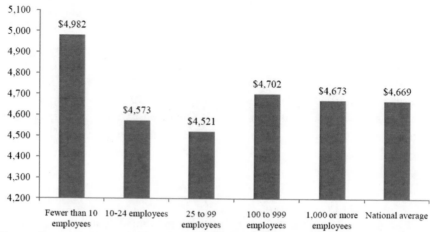

Source: Insurance Component of the Medical Expenditure Panel Survey, 2009.

Graph 6. Average Single Premium of Private Sector Employees Enrolled in an Employer-Sponsored Health Insurance Plan, by firm size, 2009.

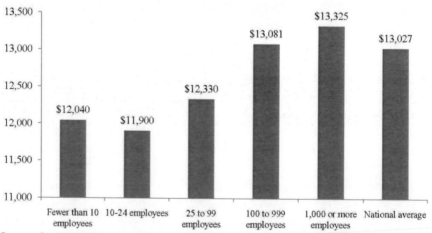

Source: Insurance Component of the Medical Expenditure Panel Survey, 2009.

Graph 7. Average Family Premium of Private Sector Employees Enrolled in an Employer-Sponsored Health Insurance Plan, by firm size, 2009.

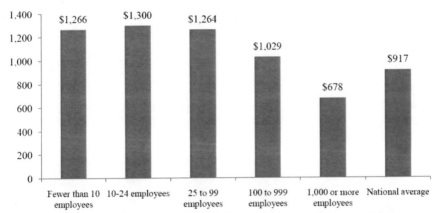

Source: Insurance Component of the Medical Expenditure Panel Survey, 2009.

Graph 8. Average Single Deductible of Private Sector Employees Enrolled in an Employer-Sponsored Health Insurance Plan, by firm size, 2009.

The 2009 MEPS data also show that the average annual deductible paid for health insurance coverage by employees varies significantly by firm size.[38] Graph 8 shows the average single deductible by firm size and Graph 9 shows the average family deductible by firm size. Graph 8 shows that, in 2009, the average single deductible for private sector employees with employer-sponsored health insurance coverage was $917. However, for employees of firms with fewer than 10 employees, the average single deductible was $1,266 and, for employees of firms with 1,000 or more employees, the average single deductible was $678. Graph 9 shows a similar pattern for family coverage, with an average family deductible of $1,761 across all firms, but an average family deductible of $2,832 for employees of firms with fewer than 10 employees and an average family deductible of $1,477 for employees of firms with 1,000 or more employees.

The MEPS data also show that the percentage of employees making a copayment for a doctor's office visit and the average amount of the copayment varies by firm size. In 2009, for firms with fewer than 10 employees, 72.5 percent of employees with health insurance were required to make a copayment for a doctor's office visit and the average copayment was $24.16.[39] For firms with 1,000 or more employees, 69.9 percent of employees were required to make a copayment for a doctor's office visit and the average copayment was $20.53 dollars. The average coinsurance for a doctor's office visit also varied by firm size, with an average coinsurance percentage of 20.6 percent for firms with fewer than 10 employees and an average coinsurance percentage of 18.1 percent for firms with 1,000 or more employees.

B. Barriers to Offering Health Insurance in Small Businesses

A 2009 report examined some of the barriers to offering health insurance that small employers face.[40] Among the barriers, the chapter identified four factors (1) low-wage workers, (2) rating and risk practices, (3) higher costs, and (4) uncertainty of future costs—as the problems small employers face. These barriers pose significant obstacles to small employers that would like to offer health insurance to their workers.

These barriers can influence the responsiveness of small employers to premium subsidies offered to encourage small businesses to offer health insurance to employees.

1. Small Business Employees are Lower Paid Than Employees of Larger Businesses

According to the National Compensation Survey (NCS), employees of small businesses earn less in benefits and in cash wages compared to employees of large businesses.[41] In general, employees who have lower wages are less likely to have health insurance through their employers. The lower paid an employee, the more likely that the employee will value cash wages over a benefit such as health insurance. In addition, some of these lower paid workers may be eligible for Medicaid or Medicare coverage, which would reduce their demand for employer-sponsored health insurance.

However, as discussed earlier, employee take-up rates tend to be reasonably uniform across firm size, suggesting that employees do generally value employer health insurance coverage.

For March 2010, private sector workers earned, on average, $27.73 per hour (or approximately $58,000 annually) including cash wages and benefits.[42] Cash wages account for approximately 70 percent of these compensation costs.[43] Table 6 shows the breakdown of average compensation costs by size of employer. The table shows a clear positive correlation between the employment size of a firm and the compensation paid to employees of the firm.

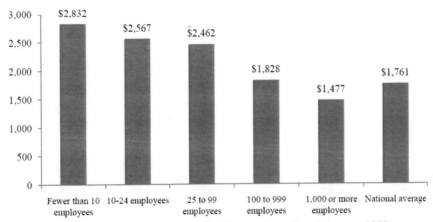

Source: Insurance Component of the Medical Expenditure Panel Survey, 2009.

Graph 9. Average Family Deductible of Private Sector Employees Enrolled in an Employer-Sponsored Health Insurance Plan, by firm size, 2009.

Table 6 – Private Sector Employer Compensation Costs in the United States, by Establishment Size, March 2010
(Average Hourly Wages)

Establishment Size, by employment	Total Compensation	Wages and Salaries	Percent of Total Compensation	Health Insurance	Percent of Total Compensation
1-49	$22.10	$16.41	74	$1.34	6
50-99	$25.10	$18.05	72	$1.82	7
100-499	$28.56	$19.99	70	$2.36	8
500 or more	$39.78	$26.45	66	$3.38	8
All firms	$27.73	$19.58	71	$2.08	8

Source: BLS, National Compensation Survey, March 2010

The lower compensation cost for health insurance for small firms relative to larger firms reflects the fact that small firms are less likely to offer health insurance as a benefit to employees.

Graph 10 displays the average hourly wages of private sector workers.[44] Employees in the smallest firms (1 to 49 workers) earn 66 cents to the dollar compared to the earnings of workers in the largest firms (500 or more workers).

Lower wage employees of small business tend to value wages over benefits. Lower income workers tend to be liquidity constrained in their household budgets, struggling to cover the household obligations. Faced with reducing their take-home paycheck by to obtain health insurance coverage, many low-income workers would prefer wages to benefits.[45]

In addition to the fact that employees of small businesses earn less, on average, than employees of large firms, the demographics of small business employees may make them less likely to value health insurance benefits over cash wages. A 2000 paper examining the demographics of small business employees found that small firms employ more workers under age 25 and more workers age 65 or older compared to large firms.[46] Those workers age 65 or older have health insurance coverage through Medicare, making this workplace benefit less important to them.

In addition, small firms have higher percentages of employees who had less than a high school diploma and employees whose highest degree was a high school diploma. Small firms employ more people who are receiving financial assistance (excluding loans) from friends or relatives and more people who receive public assistance from the government.

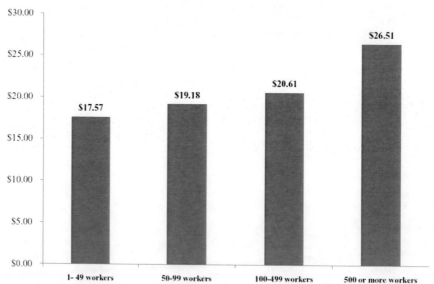

Source: Bureau of Labor Statistics, Occupational Earnings Tables: United States, December 2008 to January 2010.

Graph 10. Mean Hourly Earnings of Workers in Private Industry Establishments, by employment size of establishment.

Each of these demographic characteristics (younger and older workers, less educated workers, lower-income workers) identify classes of employees who may place less value on employer-provided health insurance than other employees.[47] As a result, employees of small businesses may generally place less value on health insurance as a benefit.

A 2010 Urban Institute study found that there are racial and ethnic differences in health insurance coverage rates explained partially by employment patterns.[48] In particular, the study found that Latino parents were more likely to have a small-firm employer or to be a contingent worker or an employee in alternative work arrangements. As a result, this study found that for Hispanic workers, this contributed to a significantly lower rate of employer-sponsored health insurance coverage (32.5 percent) relative to all groups (57.1 percent).[49]

2. Risk Group Too Small/Potential for Adverse Risk Selection

Historically, small business employers have had more difficulty finding affordable health insurance because they are unable to utilize the economies of scale that a large employer can utilize to spread risks across its workforce. A small employer's risk group is too small and the health costs of any single employee can drive up the group's average costs significantly enough to make future costs unaffordable. Sometimes, small employers can find trade association or other groups to join to enable the employer to take advantage of a large group insurance rate, but the employer must take the time to research the available groups.

Some states have changed their laws to encourage the pooling of small businesses for health insurance purposes to provide cross-subsidies among small employers, thereby reducing the problem of a single high-cost worker driving up an employer's costs substantially. At the national level, the health insurance exchanges for small businesses enacted as part of health care reform were designed to address this problem.

A related problem is the potential for adverse risk selection. Because the costs of health insurance can be quite high for a small group, only those employees who anticipate high health insurance expenses will join the group and healthy employees will opt not to purchase health insurance or to purchase such insurance separately. A recent analysis of potential problems with the health exchanges enacted as part of health care reform provides an example of adverse selection.[50] The analysis discusses a small-business pool called PacAdvantage, which operated in California from 1993 to 2006, which at one point had 150,000 enrollees. However, the pool ultimately ceased operations because it attracted enrollees with high medical costs; as sicker individuals enrolled in the pool, premiums went up, and healthier individuals left the pool for sources of less expensive insurance.

3. Higher Administrative Costs

Small employers often do not offer health insurance to their employees because of the high administrative and overhead costs of providing such coverage. In a large employer, these costs are averaged over a much larger workforce and the per employee cost of offering health insurance is relatively low. However, the administrative costs are not proportionately smaller for small businesses; as a result, small employers must average high administrative costs over a much smaller pool of employees. In addition, because job turnover tends to be higher among small employers, the ongoing administrative costs of health insurance plan elections and enrollment can be disproportionately higher than for a large employer with a more stable workforce.

The 2003 Small Business Administration study cited previously also examined the effect of administrative costs on the health insurance premium costs of small firms.[51] The study found that administrative expenses for insurers of small firm health insurance plans make up 25 to 27 percent of premiums and 33 to 37 percent of claims, compared to 5 to 11 percent for large companies with self-insured health plans.

4. Unpredictable Costs

For a small business, health insurance coverage represents a cost that is more volatile and more difficult to control than other compensation costs.[52] As a percentage of total costs, this unpredictability often presents unacceptable risks to a small business compared to a larger business. Once a business offers compensation in the form of health benefits, the business will tend to attract employees who value the benefit. Thus, it can become more difficult for the employer to discontinue the benefit.

C. Effects of the Recession on the Availability of Employer-Provided Health Insurance

Employers provide employer-sponsored health insurance to their employees as part of an overall compensation package. As noted above, economists believe that the cost of health insurance coverage provided by an employer is ultimately borne by the worker in the form of foregone wages. Further, over the long term, market forces will drive the amount that employers are willing to pay for wages and benefits. Thus, when the economy is expanding and business profits increase, employers are able to pay more to their employees in the form of wages and benefits. Conversely, during a recession when the economy is contracting, the amount that employers have available for wages and benefits will also contract. This contraction will result in reductions in (1) the size of the workforce, (2) wages paid, and (3) benefits, such as health insurance, provided to employees.

Because the provision of health insurance coverage occurs predominantly through the workforce, there is a high correlation between the lack of health insurance and the unemployment rate. A 2009 Kaiser Family Foundation analysis examines the effect of increasing unemployment on the number of individuals without health insurance.[53] In this analysis, Holahan and Garrett estimated that a one percentage point increase in unemployment would increase Medicaid enrollment by 1.0 million individuals and would increase the number of uninsured individuals by 1.1 million. Thus, in January 2009, the authors estimated that, if the unemployment rate reached 10 percent, individuals with employer-sponsored health insurance would decrease by 13.2 million, the number of individuals with Medicaid and SCHIP coverage would increase by 5.4 million, and the number of uninsured would increase by 5.8 million.[54]

Thus, one empirical question is the extent to which the recession that began in December of 2007 has affected employer-provided health insurance access and coverage. Reductions in access to employer-provided health insurance can occur (1) as employees lose their jobs and (2) as employers eliminate or alter these benefits to reduce costs. Employers could drop their employer-sponsored health insurance, increase copayments and deductibles, or alter the eligibility requirements for the health insurance.

A May 2010 Employee Benefits Research Institute (EBRI) issue brief explored changes in employment-based health insurance coverage during the most recent recession using data from the 2004 and 2008 panels of the Survey of Income and Program Participation (SIPP).[55] The EBRI issue brief found that, between December 2007 and May 2008, the percentage of workers with employment-based health coverage in their own name fell from 60.4 percent to 56.8 percent and declined further to 55.9 percent by July 2009.[56] This is consistent with the recently released Census Bureau CPS data that indicates the percent of private sector employees receiving workplace health insurance coverage decreased to 55.8 percent in 2009.

The EBRI study also looked at the decline in employment-based health insurance coverage by firm size. The study found that, from September 2007 to April 2009, there was a decline in employment-based health insurance coverage of 10.7 percent for firms with less than 25 employees, a decline of 6.9 percent for firms with 25 to 99 employees and a decline of 3.5 percent for firms with 100 or more employees. Thus, employees of small businesses faced a significantly larger decline in employment-based health coverage during this period, as shown in Graph 11.

Graph 12 shows the trends in access rates for establishments from 1998-2009 by employment size of the firms of which the establishments are a part.

For establishments in the largest class of small employers (firms with 100 to 499 employees) access rates during the period ranged from 92.7 percent to 94.8 percent. Only 33.6 percent of establishments for firms with fewer than 10 employees offered coverage in 2009 compared to 35.6 percent in 2008. Likewise, 62.5 percent of establishments for firms with 10 to 24 employees offered coverage in 2009 compared to 66.1 percent in 2008.

In the case of establishments associated with the smallest firms (fewer than 10 employees), access rates declined from a high of 39.6 in 2000 to 33.6 percent in 2009. Other small-firm establishments faced similar declines in access rates from a high of 69.9 percent in 1999 to 62.5 percent in 2009 (in the case of establishments for firms with 10 to 24 employees). For firms with 25 to 99 employees, access rates declined from a high of 85.3 percent in 1999 to 81.6 percent in 2009. Graph 12 shows this pattern of decreased access rates following the 2001 recession, for all but the largest small-employer size category. However, the decline in access rates from 2008 to 2009 is greater in all cases.

The following maps show the change in employer health insurance access rates from 2006 to 2009 for different size categories of small employers, identifying whether the access rates increased or decreased.

Overall, there were no situations where offer rates remained unchanged during this period. The lack of stability in the offer rate may reflect the relatively higher turnover rates for smaller firms. Smaller firms compared to larger firms tend to remain in business, on average, for shorter periods. Further, newer firms starting in business tend not to offer health insurance until the firm becomes established. Therefore, with this type of underlying firm turnover, it is likely that these numbers would change over time.

Map 1 shows the change in access rates for the establishments associated with the smallest firms. The vast majority of states experienced a (modest) decline in access rates, with only 17 states posting an increase.

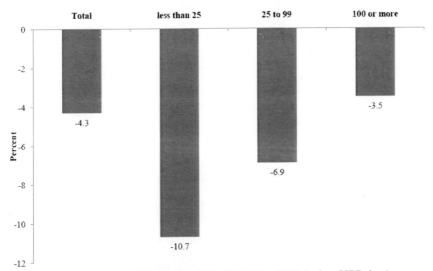

Source: Fronstin, Paul, EBRI Issue Brief No. 342, May 2010 (using SIPP data).

Graph 11. Percent Decline in Employment-Based Health Insurance Coverage, Establishment Size by Employment, September 2007 to April 2009.

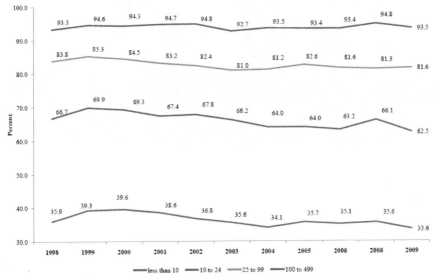

Source: DHHS, MEPS, Tables II A.2, various years.

Graph 12. Percent of Private-Sector Establishments that Offer Health Insurance, Establishments by Employment Size of Firm, 1998 to 2009.

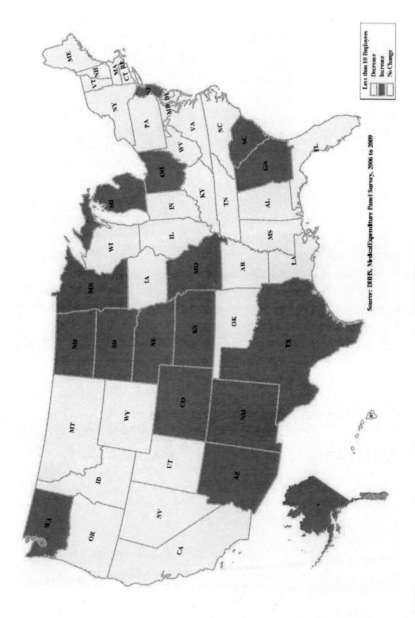

Map 1. Change in the percent of Private-Sector Establishment that Offered Health Insurance, Firm Size of Fewer than 10 Employees, 2006-2009.

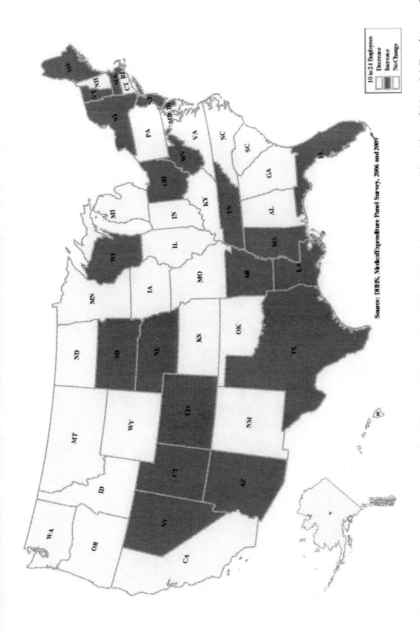

Map 2. Change in the Number of Private-Sector Establishments that Offered Health Insurance, Firm Size of 10 to 24 Employees, 2006-2009.

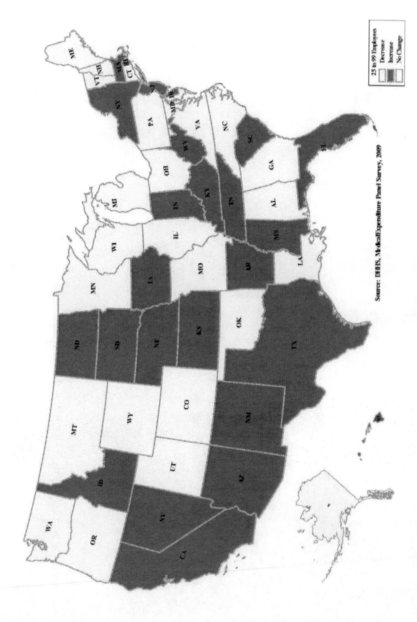

Map 3. Change in the Number of Private-Sector Establishments that Offered Health Insurance, Firm Size of 25 to 99 Employees, 2006-2009.

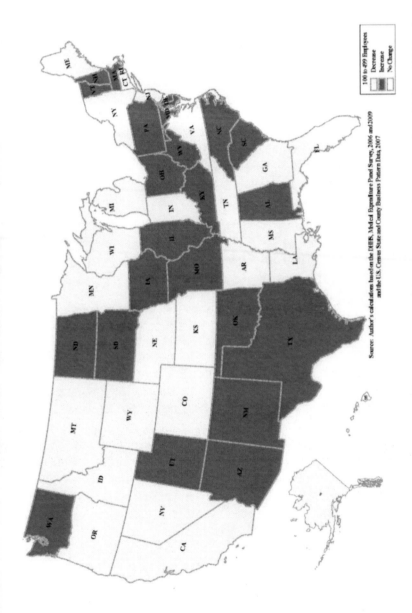

Source: Author's calculations based on the IHIIS, Medical Expenditure Panel Survey, 2006 and 2009 and the U.S. Census State and County Business Pattern Data, 2007

100 to 499 Employees

Decrease
Increase
No Change

Map 4. Change in the Number of Private-Sector Establishments that Offere Health Insurance, Firm Size of 100 to 499 Employees, 2006-2009.

A similar trend as that shown in the first map appears in Map 2 and Map 3. In both maps, the majority of states display a decrease in access. However, it is important to note that the number of states with an overall increase in access appears positively associated with firm size. Establishments associated with 10 to 24 employee firms show increases in access in 20 states and establishments associated 25 to 99 employee firms show increases in access in 25 states.

Map 4 shows the change in access rates for establishments associated with 100 to 499 employee firms. In this case, 23 states posted an increase in access over this period. Closer examination reveals that states reporting access declines had only modest declines (an average of 3.5 percent). Conversely, states reporting access increases had somewhat larger increases (an average of 4.8 percent).

IV. ANALYZING THE OFFERING OF HEALTH INSURANCE BY SMALL BUSINESSES AT THE STATE LEVEL

A. Overview

Generally, there are variations in health insurance coverage on a state-by-state basis. Certain areas of the country (the Northeast, for example) have historically had higher levels of health insurance coverage, while other areas (the Southwest, for example) have historically had lower levels of health insurance coverage.

The offering of small business health insurance coverage also varies on a state-to-state basis. Some states have higher rates of small businesses offering health insurance to employees, while other states have significantly lower offer rates. This section provides an overview of the offering of health insurance by small employers on a state-by-state basis and then explores the role that special tax incentives might play in this area.

The MEPS provides the best data on health insurance access rates by employers broken down by firm size, by state, and by other worker demographic characteristics. The data confirm that offering health insurance correlates positively with firm size. The larger the firm, the more likely it is that employees have access to health insurance. Graph 13 shows the percentage of private sector firms that offer health insurance by employer size for 1998-2009. Note that the Department of Health and Human Services (DHHS) did not conduct the Medical Expenditure Panel Survey-Insurance Component (MEPS-IC) in 2007.

The data show that the offer rates in establishments for the smallest firms (fewer than 10 employees) range from a high offer rate of 40 percent in 2000 to a low offer rate of 34 percent in 2004 and 2009. Establishments for firms with 10 to 24 employees range from a high offer rate of 70 percent in 1999 to a low of 63 percent in 2006 and 2009. Establishments for firms with 25 to 99 employees range from an offer rate of 85 percent in 1999 and 2000 to a low of 81 percent in 2003, 2004, and 2008. The two largest firm size categories (100-999 employees and 1,000 or more employees) have comparable establishment offer rates of approximately 95 percent and 99 percent, respectively. This is consistent with the notion that larger, more established firms are unlikely to drop their employer-provided health insurance programs.

Health insurance offer rates also show significant geographic variation. Table 7 provides the establishment access rates by firm size and by state for 2009.

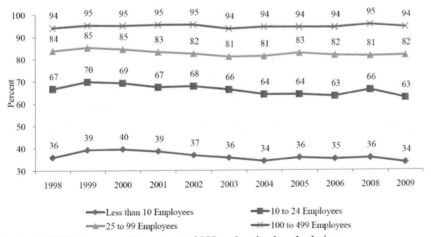

Source: MEPS, Insurance Component, 2009 and author's calculations.

Graph 13. Establishment Offer Rates for Health Insurance, by Employment Size of Firm, 1998-2009.

Table 7. Offer Rates for Employer-Provided Health Insurance, 2009
(Percent of establishments, by firm size and by state)

	Less than 10 employees	10-24 employees	25-99 employees	100-499 employees†
Alabama	34	58	88	91
Alaska	20	42	64	94
Arizona	31	38	76	95
Arkansas	23	43	72	93
California	37	62	82	89
Colorado	38	62	84	91
Connecticut	44	74	92	97
Delaware	38	68	86	88
District of Columbia	55	74	87	100
Florida	27	67	79	94
Georgia	30	53	79	87
Hawaii	76	96	99	98
Idaho	26	53	75	94
Illinois	31	64	85	94
Indiana	23	43	79	92
Iowa	28	59	90	96
Kansas	33	62	86	91
Kentucky	29	66	86	95
Louisiana	23	52	73	88
Maine	33	76	86	99
Maryland	42	68	84	95
Massachusetts	40	76	91	99
Michigan	33	64	85	93
Minnesota	36	60	75	97
Mississippi	21	57	78	88
Missouri	32	67	80	98
Montana	22	57	77	97
Nebraska	24	50	77	94
Nevada	30	60	75	87
New Hampshire	39	76	89	98
New Jersey	50	77	90	99
New Mexico	27	55	72	91
New York	44	74	90	93
North Carolina	24	63	76	97
North Dakota	30	64	91	93

	Less than 10 employees	10-24 employees	25-99 employees	100-499 employees†
Ohio	42	72	82	97
Oklahoma	24	51	77	93
Oregon	35	54	83	92
Pennsylvania	42	66	85	98
Rhode Island	43	69	96	95
South Carolina	28	58	78	94
South Dakota	29	70	81	98
Tennessee	29	57	86	92
Texas	28	53	68	90
Utah	24	54	73	93
Vermont	38	82	91	100
Virginia	28	66	81	98
Washington	34	64	84	97
West Virginia	25	54	77	90
Wisconsin	25	61	88	91
Wyoming	22	53	72	90

† Authors' calculations. Estimated access rates rely on the MEPS-IC, 2009 and the U.S. Census State and County Business Patterns, 2007. MEPS-IC does not provide a breakdown for firms with 100 to 499 employees. Thus, we estimated weights, based on employment statistics from Census State and County Business Patterns, for the firm size of 100 to 499 employees to derive the appropriate access rates.

Access rates for employer-sponsored health insurance tend to follow regional patterns. Access rates tend to be higher in Northeastern states and lower in Southwestern states. Some states with higher-than-average offer rates among small employers have special programs designed to make health insurance more affordable to small businesses. For example, New York has the Healthy NY program, which is a subsidized reinsurance pool providing lower cost health insurance for low-income individuals and small businesses with 50 or fewer employees.[57] The geographical differences in offer rates likely reflect a variety of factors, including: (1) some states may maintain programs designed to encourage small businesses to offer health insurance, (2) employers in geographic areas compete for the same employees and, therefore, are likely to offer similar benefit packages and (3) there may be higher concentrations of employers that are less likely to offer health insurance in certain geographic areas, such as less populous areas and rural areas.[58]

B. The Role of Special Tax Incentives at the State Level in the Offering of Small Business Health Insurance

One question that we examined is whether there is a relationship between state-by-state variations in the offering of small business health insurance and the adoption of special state tax incentives to encourage small businesses to offer health insurance to employees. Table 8 shows that relatively few states adopted state tax incentives for health insurance.[59] Appendix C provides a more complete listing of the special provisions applicable to health insurance and small businesses in all 50 states and the District of Columbia.

Table 8. State Tax Incentives for Small Businesses to Offer Health Insurance to Employees, 2009

State	Type of Tax Incentive
Alabama	Permits businesses with less than 25 employees to deduct 150 percent of the amount paid for employee health insurance premiums. This deduction took effect beginning in 2009. Employees of eligible employers may deduct 50 percent of the amount they paid for health insurance premiums.
Arizona	Provides an indirect incentive for small business health insurance by allowing health insurers a credit against premium taxes for up to 50 percent of premiums (up to $1,000 per single individual and $3,000 per family) received from small businesses (businesses with 2-25 employees).
Georgia	Georgia provides up to $250 per year per enrolled employee (nonrefundable) tax credit for small business high-deductible health insurance plans. Small business is defined as a business with 1-50 employees. This credit took effect beginning in 2009.
Idaho	Provides a tax credit for employer-provided health insurance for new employees who are provided health insurance (if average employment increases over the prior year). The credit is $1,000 for employees earning at least $15.50 per hour and $500 for other employees.
Indiana	Indiana allows businesses (with 2-100 employees) to claim a 50 percent credit for the costs of providing qualified wellness programs to employees.
Kansas	Kansas provides a refundable small business health insurance credit for up to 3 years. Credit equals $70 per month per enrolled employee in year one, $50 in year two, and $35 in year three. An eligible small business has between 2 and 50 employees and has not contributed to any health insurance premium or Health Savings Account for employees for the prior two years. This health insurance credit was

State	Type of Tax Incentive
	effective beginning in 2005; prior to 2005, a smaller credit was available.
Maine	Maine allows a nonrefundable credit for employers with no more than 5 employees for dependent health insurance provided to low-income employees. Credit is 20 percent of dependent health benefits or $125 per year up to 50 percent of state income tax liability. Low-income employees must work at least 30 hours per week or 1,000 hours per year.
Missouri	Missouri provides a self-employed health insurance tax credit to taxpayers who are not eligible for the Federal self-employed health insurance deduction.
Montana	Montana permits small business employers with 20 or fewer employees working at least 20 hours per week to claim a nonrefundable tax credit for up to 3 years if the employer pays at least 50 percent of each Montana employee's health insurance premiums. The maximum credit is $25 per month per employee up to 10 employees or $250. If the employer pays less than 100 percent of the health insurance premiums, the amount of the credit is proportionately reduced. Montana enacted the credit in its current form in 2001. Employers with 2-9 employees who provide health insurance to their employees and do not receive premium assistance through the small business health insurance pool may claim a separate refundable credit against corporation income tax. The credit is up to $100 per month per employee, $100 per employee's spouse, and $40 per employee's dependent (up to a maximum of 50 percent of premiums paid). This credit is part of the Insure Montana program, funded by and subject to tobacco tax revenues. The program was at capacity in 2009.
North Carolina	Effective for 2007-2009, small businesses with no more than 25 employees are eligible to claim a small business health insurance credit against North Carolina corporate or personal income tax or corporation franchise tax. The employer must pay at least 50 percent of the employee premiums. The credit is available with respect to employees whose total annual wages do not exceed $40,000. The maximum per employee credit is $250. The credit sunsetted for taxable years beginning after December 31, 2009.
Oklahoma	Oklahoma provides a refundable tax credit to employers. The employer must offer new health insurance coverage to employees and pay at least 50 percent of the premium for employees. Credit is $15 per month per eligible employee for up to 2 years. An eligible employee must work an average of 24 hours per week or more. Oklahoma also has a premium assistance program available to employers with less than 100 employees to provide assistance with health insurance expenses of eligible low-income employees.

Sources: National Council of State Legislatures and various state legislative websites.

An interesting question is whether the experiences in the states might lend any insight into the general question of the effectiveness of tax incentives to encourage small businesses to offer health insurance to their employees. The approaches in the states vary widely. There is no single type of special tax incentive adopted by the states. In general, the provisions adopted are available to different categories of small businesses. These special tax incentives generally have been limited to the smallest employers. Some programs are available to employers with less than 20 employees and some are available to employers with fewer than 10 employees. In addition, in some cases, the type of tax incentive provided is relatively narrow. Indiana, for example, provides a tax incentive only for the provision of qualified wellness programs. Arizona provides an indirect incentive to small businesses by providing a premium tax credit for insurers selling health insurance to small businesses. Some of the state programs, like Alabama, have only been in effect for a short time, thus providing an insufficient time to test the effectiveness of the state's incentives.

This section examines the tax incentives adopted in two states – Kansas and Montana – in order to explore whether there is any evidence of the effectiveness of these special tax incentives in encouraging small businesses to offer health insurance to their employees. These states have the broadest tax incentives adopted and have maintained these incentives for sufficient time to examine the potential affect on offer rates.

1. Kansas

Kansas offers a refundable small business health insurance credit to eligible small businesses for up to 3 years. Refundable credits are essentially equivalent to a direct subsidy payment from the state government because the credit is available without regard to the business's tax liability. A refundable tax credit provides a dollar-for-dollar subsidy as opposed to a deduction in which the value of the tax subsidy is determined by the marginal income tax rate faced by the taxpayer.

The Kansas small employer tax credit equals $70 per month ($840 per year) per enrolled employee in year one, $50 per month ($600 per year) in year two, and $35 per month ($420 per year) in year three. A small business is eligible for this credit if it has between 2 and 50 employees and has not contributed to any health insurance premium or Health Savings Account for employees for the prior two years. New businesses that have been in existence for less than two years are also eligible if they have not provided health insurance or Health Savings Accounts to their employees.

For 2009, the average premium per enrolled employee for employer-based health insurance in the state of Kansas was $4,236 ($353 per month) for single coverage and $11,829 ($986 per month) for family coverage.[60] Thus, the $70 per month small employer credit provides a subsidy equal to approximately 20 percent of the average cost of single health insurance coverage provided through employer-sponsored insurance and approximately 7 percent of the average cost of family health insurance coverage.

The Kansas credit is interesting for two reasons. First, the current iteration of the credit has been in effect since 2005. Second, there was a smaller credit in effect for the years 2000-2005. By looking at employer health insurance access rates in the state of Kansas, it may be possible to determine whether the small employer health insurance credit had any discernible impact on the small employer health insurance access rate in the state. In addition, the Kansas credit is only available to employers that have not offered health insurance for the prior two years. It is important to remember that this analysis is imprecise because there are other factors, such as general economic conditions and other legislation relating to the offering of health insurance that might also affect the small employer access rates.

The Department of Health and Human Services, Agency for Healthcare Research and Quality did not collect data for 2001 for the state of Kansas and did not conduct the MEPS for 2007. Offer rates for Kansas employer health insurance tend to the middle range of access rates nationwide (see Tables 8 through 11).

Table 9. Access Rates for Employer-Provided Health Insurance in Kansas, 2000-2009, Percent of Establishments, by Firm Size

Firm Size, by employment	2000	2001	2002	2003	2004	2005	2006	2007	2008	2009
Less than 10	39	n/a	34	33	34	29	32	n/a	36	33
10-24	71	n/a	59	66	58	63	62	n/a	71	62
25-99	91	n/a	68	83	83	85	83	n/a	77	86
100-999	90	n/a	91	95	95	92	94	n/a	96	92
1,000 or more	99	n/a	100	100	98	100	98	n/a	100	99

Source: Tabulations from Department of Health and Human Services, Agency for Healthcare Research and Quality, Medical Expenditure Panel Survey, various years. The complete file for all states and all employer sizes is located in Appendix A.

Establishment access rates did not demonstrate a discernible uptick after the increased tax credit went into effect in Kansas in 2005. In fact, the only discernible pattern in the access rates appears to be in 2002, when there was a noticeable decline in access rates for employers with fewer than 100 employees, which may be a response to the recession that began in 2001. In 2009, there was a decline in access rates for the two smallest classes of employers, which may be attributable to the most recent recession.

2. *Montana*

Historically, the health insurance access rate by small businesses in the state of Montana has been among the lowest rates in the country. In 2009, only 22 percent of the establishments for firms with fewer than 10 employees in Montana offered health insurance to their employees and the overall access rate for all establishments in the state was approximately 40 percent, the lowest access rate in the country.[61]

The state of Montana has a two-part system of incentives for small employers. There is a nonrefundable credit for employers with 20 or fewer employees and a refundable credit for employers with 2-9 employees who provide health insurance and do not receive a premium subsidy through the Montana small business purchasing pool.

Montana permits small business employers with 20 or fewer employees working at least 20 hours per week to claim a nonrefundable tax credit for up to three years if the employer pays at least 50 percent of each Montana employee's health insurance premiums. The credit equals 50 percent of the percentage of premiums paid by the employer times $25 per month per employee up to 10 employees. The maximum credit applies if the employer pays 100 percent of the premium; the maximum credit equals $250 per month or $3,000 per year. If the employer pays less than 100 percent of the health insurance premiums, the amount of the credit declines proportionately, but the credit is not available if the employer pays less than 50 percent of the premiums. Nonrefundable credits can only be used by employers with positive income tax liability. This credit has been in effect in this form since 2001.

Montana also allows employers to take a separate refundable credit against corporation income tax. This credit is available to employers with 2-9 employees who provide health insurance to their employees and do not receive premium assistance through the small business health insurance purchasing pool. The credit is up to $100 per month per employee, $100 per employee's spouse, and $40 per employee's dependent (up to a maximum of 50 percent of premiums paid). For employees who are at least age 45, the tax credit increases to $125 per month. This credit is part of the Insure Montana program, which receives funding by and is subject to tobacco tax revenues. In 2009, the Insure Montana program was at capacity with 700 businesses participating in the purchasing pool and another 700 businesses qualifying for the tax credit.[62] On July 1, 2009, an additional $3 million became available, which led to the enrollment of an additional 169 businesses in the purchasing pool program and 79 businesses in the tax credit program. There are approximately 100-150 additional businesses on a waiting list.

In 2009, the average single premium per enrolled employee in employer-provided health insurance in the state of Montana was $4,546 per year. The average premium for family coverage was $11,365.

With respect to the nonrefundable credit available to employers with up to 20 employees, the $300 annual tax credit per employee is approximately 7 percent of the annual single premium for Montana for 2009 and approximately 3 percent of the average family premium.

The separate refundable tax credit for very small employers (2-9 employees) that do not receive assistance through the state small business health insurance pool is more generous than the nonrefundable credit. The refundable credit offers a subsidy of $100 per month for a single individual ($1,200 per year) and $240 per month ($2,880) for family coverage for a married couple plus one child.

Table 10. Access Rates for Employer-Provided Health Insurance in Montana, 2000-2009, Percent of Establishments, by Firm Size

Firm Size, by employment	2000	2001	2002	2003	2004	2005	2006	2007	2008	2009
Fewer than 10	n/a	n/a	39	30	22	20	22	n/a	25	22
10-24	n/a	n/a	56	62	50	55	63	n/a	61	57
25-99	n/a	n/a	71	74	76	85	88	n/a	66	77
100-999	n/a	n/a	98	95	93	88	100	n/a	97	97
1,000 or more	n/a	n/a	91	96	95	95	100	n/a	97	100

Source: Tabulations from Department of Health and Human Services, Agency for Healthcare Research and Quality, Medical Expenditure Panel Survey, various years. The complete file for all states and all firm sizes is located in Appendix A.

Note: The Medical Expenditure Panel Survey was not conducted in 2007. While the survey was conducted in years 2000 and 2001, data for certain states is not available.

The nonrefundable credit in Montana pays up to $3,000 per year for up to three years for employers with up to 20 employees. This credit might encourage employers who do not offer health insurance coverage to offer it to their employees. On the other hand, the amount of the credit per employee ($250 per year) is such a small percentage of the average premiums for employer-sponsored health insurance that it is unlikely to provide any significant incentive for employers to offer health insurance coverage. Further, the refundable credit is available only to those employers that already provide health insurance coverage to their employees and is only available to the smallest employers (those with 2-9 employees); thus, this credit is unlikely to induce significant new health insurance offerings by small employers.

The data support this analysis. For the smallest two classes of employers (those with fewer than 10 employees and those with 10 to 24 employees), the access rates have declined or fluctuated up and down over the 2002 to 2009 period. For employers with fewer than 10 employees, the access rate for health insurance declined from 39 percent in 2002 to 22 percent in 2009. In addition, the Insure Montana program, which provides a purchasing pool to eligible employers, may also influence the access rates for employer health insurance.

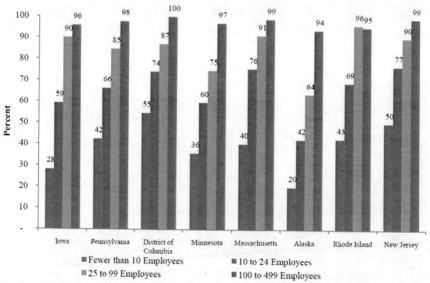

Source: Access rates from the MEPS, Insurance Component by state; state tax rate data from authors' research.

Graph 14. Small Business Health Insurance Establishment Access Rates, by Firm Size States with State Corporate Tax Rates of 9 percent or higher.

C. Relationship between State Tax Rates and Health Insurance Offer Rates

Conventional wisdom generally posits that tax rates will influence business decisions, particularly the decision to offer employee benefits. This view neglects to consider the many facets of business decision making. If businesses respond to high tax rates, then as state tax rates increase the state access rates for health insurance should theoretically decline.

From an employee's perspective, increasing tax rates provide a benefit because of the favorable tax treatment for employer-sponsored health insurance. Typically, from the small business perspective, increasing tax rates represent an increased burden to small business operations. To examine if high tax rates imposed a burden to small employers and perhaps, influenced the health insurance access rates, the analysis considers the two extremes of state corporation tax rates (states with the highest rates and zero tax states); these extremes are represented by states with corporate tax rates at 9 percent or higher and states with no corporate income tax. Graph 14 displays the eight states with corporation tax rates at 9 percent or higher. Among these states, it is noteworthy that Alaska has the lowest access rates, but otherwise the state health insurance access rates (for all small business sizes) remain high. Graph 15 displays the four states with no corporation income tax. In this graph, it is noteworthy that Wyoming has the lowest access rates (compared to the other zero-tax states as well as all states).

The graphs suggest that the small business decision to offer health insurance to their workforce depends on a number of factors and state tax rates play a small role in influencing this decision.

V. USE OF EXISTING FEDERAL TAX INCENTIVES BY SMALL BUSINESSES AND IMPLICATIONS OF HEALTH CARE REFORM

Theoretically, an employer is indifferent between offering benefits and paying wages to their employees. From a Federal tax perspective, the employer's tax treatment of a dollar of benefits is the same as a dollar of wages – the employer is entitled to a current deduction for these compensation costs.[63] As a result, the desire to attract a workforce that meets the business's needs will largely drive the employer's decision to offer a benefit such as health insurance in lieu of cash compensation.

In practice, when an employer provides health insurance benefits, it may become difficult for some employers to discontinue such benefits – despite the potential cost increases. On the other hand, wages offer predictable costs that the employer controls directly. In many ways, the employer – particularly the small employer – has little control over the health insurance costs for the workplace coverage.

Employees, on the other hand, should prefer to receive some of their compensation in the form of benefits such as health insurance because of the Federal tax benefits to an employee of receiving health insurance coverage through the employer in lieu of cash wages and lower costs with group purchases. Thus, as a rule, employees should exert pressure on employers to offer health insurance as a benefit.

Because Federal taxes represent a substantial percentage of overall tax liability for most people, the Federal tax advantage for employer-provided health insurance provides a far greater incentive than the state tax effects. Thus, the Federal tax rather than state tax effects are more likely important drivers of behavior.

The following sections examine the role of the Federal tax incentives for health insurance. One method to demonstrate the importance of Federal tax incentives is to consider what Federal tax data suggests concerning the utilization of employer-sponsored health insurance.

A. Small Corporation Use of Federal Incentives

As with other compensation, an employer is entitled to deduct the cost of health insurance premiums paid on behalf of their employees. Employers report the amounts deducted for health insurance separately from other compensation amounts. Recent corporation income tax data suggest that the deduction for all employee benefits (excluding retirement savings) was approximately $322 billion in 2007.[64] Health insurance comprises nearly 90 percent of all benefits (excluding retirement savings) for small corporations.[65] This suggests that small corporations deducted approximately $53.8 billion for health insurance benefits alone.[66]

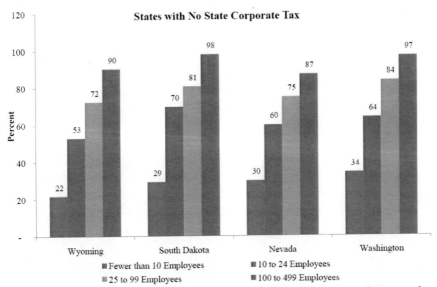

Source: Access rates from the MEPS, Insurance Component by state and tax rate data
from authors' research.

Graph 15. Small Business Health Insurance Establishment Access Rates, by Firm Size
for States with No State Corporate Tax.

While small employers file approximately 98 percent of corporation
income tax returns, they account for only 19 percent of the employee benefits
deducted.[67] Graph 16 displays the estimated amounts that small corporations
deducted for health insurance benefits. Since 2003, the amount deducted
remained approximately 19 percent of the total benefits deducted for all
corporations. However, the amount deducted for small corporations increased
11 percent from 2003 to 2007.

The employer deduction for health insurance is only one side of the story.
If the employer contributes to the cost of health insurance for their employees,
those amounts are excludable from the employee's income for both income
and payroll taxes. The Joint Committee on Taxation reported that in 2007,
individuals saved approximately $246 billion in Federal taxes for amounts
paid by their employers for health insurance.[68] This tax savings includes both
income tax ($145.3 billion) and employment taxes ($100.7 billion).

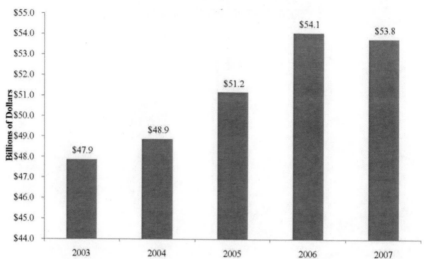

Source: Author's calculation based on Statistics of Income Corporate Source Book
Data (2003-2007) and Employer Benefit Costs From the Bureau of Labor
Statistics, National Compensation Survey.

Graph 16. Estimated Small Corporation Deduction for Employer Health Insurance
Benefits, Tax Years 2003 to 2007.

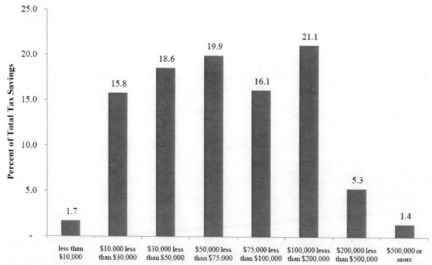

Source: Joint Committee on Taxation, JCX-66-08.

Graph 17. Total Tax Savings for the Exclusion of Health Insurance Benefits Provided
by an Employer, Distributed by Adjusted Gross Income, Tax Year 2007.

Source: Internal Revenue Service, Statistics of Income, Individual Income Tax
Returns, Table 1.4, 1998 through 2008.

Graph 18. Amount of Self-Employed Health Deduction for Returns Claiming a
Deduction, Tax Years 1998 to 2008.

Nearly 75 percent of the individual tax savings (73.2 percent) accrues to
taxpayers with adjusted gross incomes of less than $100,000, as shown in
Graph 17. In general, employees of small businesses tend to earn less
compared to their counterparts working with large employers. Therefore, it is
likely that employees of small businesses would find both the provision of
employer-sponsored insurance and the corresponding tax savings to be an
important benefit. However, as noted in Part II above, because of the
graduated Federal income tax rate structure, the value of the exclusion
becomes more valuable for individuals with higher adjusted gross income.
Thus, while 21 percent of the exclusion accrues to taxpayers in the $100,000
to $200,000 adjusted gross income category, this represents a relatively small
percentage of all taxpayers.

B. Self-Employed Use of Federal Incentives

Under current law, self-employed individuals are entitled to deduct the
costs of health insurance for themselves and their spouses and dependents. The
deduction does not apply for self-employment tax purposes, which creates a

disparity of treatment between self-employed individuals and corporate owners who work for their corporation. For many years, the deduction for self-employed health insurance expenses was 50 percent of the cost of health insurance. Legislation enacted in 1998 phased in the self-employed health insurance deduction to 60 percent for 1999 through 2001, 70 percent for 2002, and 100 percent in 2003 and thereafter.

Graph 18 shows that the annual total deductions for self-employed health insurance increased significantly between 2002 and 2003 (56.9 percent increase). This suggests that the increase in the self-employed health insurance tax deduction from 70 percent in 2002 to 100 percent in 2003 created an incentive for some self-employed individuals to purchase health insurance or perhaps purchase more insurance. In fact, the number of returns claiming the self-employed health insurance deduction increased 6.5 percent (from 3.6 to 3.8 million returns) between 2002 and 2003. (Refer to Table A1 in Appendix A for the numbers of returns and the deduction amounts.)

Source: Internal Revenue Service, Statistics of Income, Individual Income Tax Returns, Table 1.4, 2008. Averages calculated as total self-employed deductions divided by total returns claiming the deduction.

Graph 19. Average Amount of Self-Employed Health Deduction for Returns Claiming a Deduction, Tax Years 1998-2008.

Graph 19 displays the average amount of the self-employed health deduction for those returns claiming a deduction. As shown, the average deduction claimed increased 47.3 percent between 2002 and 2003. This increase in the average deduction amount indicates that the value of the deduction, the cost of health insurance, and the quantity of insurance increased. The subsequent increases, from 2004 through 2008, are consistent with increases in the cost of insurance, as the number of returns claiming the deduction decreased slightly over this period.

The deduction for self-employed health insurance tends to correlate positively with income. Unlike the exclusion for employer-sponsored insurance that delivers sizeable benefits to lower income taxpayers, the self-employed deduction distributes the tax benefits more evenly among income classes. Graph 20 distributes the returns and the amount of the self-employed deduction by adjusted gross income class. Approximately half (49 percent) of the tax benefits (deduction amounts) accrue to taxpayers with incomes over $100,000.

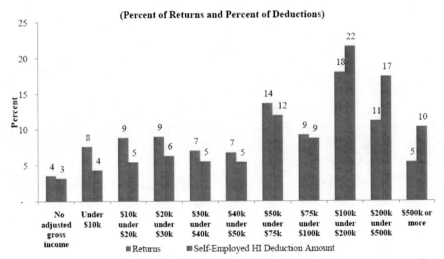

Source: Internal Revenue Service, Statistics of Income, Individual Income Tax Returns, Table 1.4, 2008.

Graph 20. Self-Employed Deduction for Health Insurance, Returns and Deduction Amount, Distributed by AGI, Tax Year 2008.

C. Health Care Reform

1. Overview

The Patient Protection and Affordable Care Act of 2010 (Health Care Reform Act), signed by President Obama on March 23, 2010, adopts significant changes to the system of health care delivery in the United States. The Act will set up state health insurance exchanges that will offer individuals and small businesses access to health insurance, provide greater regulation of health insurance, and provide tax credits for individuals and small businesses to help offset the cost of health insurance.

The Health Care Reform Act affects small businesses in a variety of ways. Small employers with 50 or more employees are assessed a fee if they do not provide health insurance to their employees and if any of their employees received subsidized health insurance coverage through a health insurance exchange. Small businesses with fewer than 50 employees are exempt from this requirement.

Beginning in 2014, small businesses with up to 100 employees will have access to health insurance through the state exchanges. Starting in 2017, states will have the option of expanding the state exchanges to businesses with more than 100 employees. In addition, employees of small businesses that do not offer health insurance will be able to purchase health insurance through the exchanges.

The Act requires the Department of Health and Human Services to establish a new website with information on affordable and comprehensive health insurance coverage choices. In addition, the website will provide specific information geared toward small businesses, such as information on using the small business tax credits and finding insurance through health exchanges. This website is located at http://www.healthcare.gov/foryou/small/index.html.

2. Small Business Health Insurance Tax Credit

One of the most significant aspects of health care reform for small businesses is the adoption of the small business health insurance tax credit. Beginning in 2010, small businesses can claim a nonrefundable tax credit for the costs of health insurance they provide to their employees.[69] As a nonrefundable credit, the credit in any year is limited to the employer's Federal income tax liability for the year. Because this credit is a general business credit, the business may carry any unused credit amount back one year and forward up to 20 years.

The tax credit is available to employers with less than 25 full-time equivalent (FTE) employees and average wages of less than $50,000 per year. The maximum credit is 35 percent of an employer's contributions to employer-sponsored insurance for 2010-2013 and 50 percent for 2014 and later years.

An employer must contribute at least 50 percent of the premium costs to qualify for this credit, but could pay up to 100 percent of the premium costs. The following examples illustrate the value of the credit.

Example 1.—Assume an employer contributes 100 percent of the premium costs for employee health insurance coverage. The employer has 10 full-time employees with average wages of $25,000, so the employer qualifies for the maximum credit of 35 percent (2010-2013) and 50 percent in 2014 and beyond. In 2010, five employees have single coverage with per employee premium costs of $5,000 and five employees have family coverage with per employee premium costs of $11,000. The employer's total premium costs are $80,000 (5×$5,000 plus 5×$11,000). The employer qualifies for the maximum credit rate of 35 percent, so the employer is eligible for a credit of $28,000 (.35×$80,000).

Example 2.—Assume the employer in Example 1 contributes 50 percent of the premium costs for employee health insurance coverage. In this case, the employer would qualify for a maximum credit of $14,000 (.35×.50 of the premium costs).

A recent study estimated the number of small employers that might be eligible for the small business health insurance tax credit.[70] These estimates are consistent with estimates of the President's Council of Economic Advisors that approximately 4 million small businesses would be eligible for the credit.[71] Table 12 shows the estimates, by state, of the number of businesses with no more than 25 employees and average wages of less than $50,000 and the estimates of the number of businesses with no more than 10 employees and average wages of less than $25,000 for 2010.

Because average wages determine eligibility for the small business health credit, there will be geographic disparities in eligibility. In states with higher average wages, fewer employers will qualify for the credit. Similarly, in states with lower average wages, more employers will qualify.

Two factors will affect actual utilization of the credit. First, for a variety of reasons, it is likely that the credit will initially primarily benefit those small businesses that already provide health insurance for their employees. Some

Quantria Strategies LLC

small employers may be reluctant to offer health insurance to their employees because of perceived uncertainty about the effects of health care reform. Other small employers may wait until the health insurance exchanges are available to offer health insurance to their employees. Because of uncertainty about the economy, other small employers may defer decisions to add a new employee benefit.

Table 12. Estimated Number of Small Businesses with Fewer Than 25 (10) Employees and Average Wages of Less Than $50,000 ($25,000), 2010

State	Total Number of Businesses with 25 or Fewer Employees	Employers with 25 or Fewer Employees and Less than $50,000 Average Wages		Employers with 10 or Fewer Employees and Less than $25,000 Average Wages	
		Number	Percent of Total	Number	Percent of Total
Alabama	57,800	50,600	87.7	15,900	27.5
Alaska	12,800	10,400	81.0	3,700	28.9
Arizona	84,700	72,600	85.7	18,900	22.3
Arkansas	42,300	39,900	94.2	13,000	30.7
California	571,200	456,500	79.9	135,900	23.8
Colorado	99,700	82,400	82.6	24,500	24.6
Connecticut	57,500	44,000	76.5	12,900	22.4
Delaware	13,700	11,300	82.7	3,100	22.6
District of Columbia	11,800	6,800	57.8	1,500	12.7
Florida	307,100	246,000	80.1	77,400	25.2
Georgia	143,200	120,300	84.0	37,500	26.2
Hawaii	20,100	16,300	81.3	4,900	24.4
Idaho	33,200	29,800	89.5	10,400	31.3
Illinois	203,600	159,900	78.5	48,400	23.8
Indiana	94,800	88,100	92.9	26,000	27.4
Iowa	56,300	51,100	90.8	14,000	24.9
Kansas	51,600	45,800	88.9	13,100	25.4
Kentucky	57,400	51,500	89.2	15,800	27.5
Louisiana	66,200	57,400	86.8	18,800	28.4
Maine	28,700	25,800	90.1	8,600	30.0
Maryland	82,600	66,000	79.8	18,500	22.4
Massachusetts	109,700	81,300	74.1	19,800	18.1
Michigan	148,300	126,300	85.1	39,600	26.7
Minnesota	92,500	77,900	84.3	22,800	24.7

State	Total Number of Businesses with 25 or Fewer Employees	Employers with 25 or Fewer Employees and Less than $50,000 Average Wages		Employers with 10 or Fewer Employees and Less than $25,000 Average Wages	
		Number	Percent of Total	Number	Percent of Total
Mississippi	36,600	34,100	93.2	11,400	31.3
Missouri	92,700	85,100	91.8	25,100	27.1
Montana	28,800	27,100	94.0	8,300	28.8
Nebraska	35,400	33,200	93.8	10,300	29.1
Nevada	38,100	29,600	77.8	9,400	24.7
New Hampshire	24,400	19,600	80.3	4,500	18.4
New Jersey	163,500	126,800	77.5	37,000	22.6
New Mexico	27,900	24,800	88.9	5,500	19.7
New York	349,500	285,000	81.6	78,300	22.4
North Carolina	144,200	126,100	87.5	37,600	26.1
North Dakota	16,500	15,200	91.9	5,100	30.9
Ohio	149,100	127,800	85.7	38,900	26.1
Oklahoma	58,400	50,300	86.2	18,200	31.2
Oregon	77,000	67,100	87.1	19,800	25.7
Pennsylvania	178,500	160,700	90.0	43,800	24.5
Rhode Island	19,100	15,700	82.0	3,900	20.4
South Carolina	60,400	53,200	88.1	15,900	26.3
South Dakota	18,800	17,600	93.6	4,600	24.5
Tennessee	74,200	66,500	89.6	21,600	29.1
Texas	307,800	248,700	80.8	79,100	25.7
Utah	44,200	37,800	85.5	12,600	28.5
Vermont	14,900	13,100	87.9	3,400	22.8
Virginia	127,000	102,600	80.8	30,700	24.2
Washington	127,200	110,000	86.5	32,500	25.6
West Virginia	23,500	21,200	90.3	6,100	26.0
Wisconsin	99,200	86,100	86.8	25,800	26.0
Wyoming	15,600	12,700	86.8	4,000	25.6
Total, U.S.	4,798,300	4,015,300	83.7	1,198,700	25.0

Source: Lewin Group estimates for Families USA and Small Business Majority, 2010. These estimates are consistent with estimates of the President's Council of Economic Advisors that approximately 4 million small businesses would be eligible for the credit. See http://www.treasury.gov/press-center/press-releases/ Documents/additional%20background%20on%20the%20small%20business%20h ealth%20care%20tax%20credit.pdf.

Second, it is important to remember that only those employers with positive Federal tax liability will be able to utilize the credit in the current year. If an employer does not have sufficient Federal tax liability, the credit is not currently available and the employer must carry over and use the credit to offset Federal income tax liability in subsequent years (or can carry any unused amount back one year).

According to the 2007 IRS Statistics of Income (SOI), approximately 42.8 percent of all small businesses (businesses with assets of less than $10 million) filing a corporate return (including S corporations) have no net income and therefore, no Federal tax liability.[72] However, those small businesses likely to offer health insurance benefits to their workers are also more likely to report net income. Further, in the early years following availability of the credit, it is likely that those firms that previously offered health insurance benefits will claim the vast majority of the tax credits. There are three possible responses of small employers to the health insurance tax credit and the other provisions of health care reform: (1) small employers that either offer health insurance to their employees currently or do not offer such coverage continue the status quo, (2) small employers that offer health insurance to their employees drop the coverage, and (3) small employers who do not currently offer health insurance to their employees begin to offer it. In the short run, the possible responses in (1) (i.e., the status quo response) may be the most likely response as employers take time to evaluate the effects of health care reform legislation and to analyze the costs and benefits of offering health insurance to employees. The status quo response will tend to result in utilization of the credit by those employers already offering health insurance to their employees. On the other hand, there is considerable uncertainty about the possible take-up rates for small employer health insurance under health care reform. The Congressional Budget Office estimated that approximately 1 million fewer people would have employer-based health insurance coverage in 2019-2021 because of health care reform.[73] However, this estimate reflects the net effect of individuals having new access to employer health insurance, having access to employer health insurance but enrolling in an exchange health plan instead, or losing access to employer health insurance.

Estimates of the number of small businesses eligible for the health insurance tax credit identify the potential universe of small businesses eligible for the credit, but do not account for the fact that not all small businesses would be able to utilize the credit because they do not have sufficient Federal tax liability to benefit from the credit. The ability to utilize the credit will affect the attractiveness of the credit for many small businesses.

Our estimates suggest that the actual number of small businesses that could benefit from the credit will be much smaller than the 4 million estimated to be eligible for it. Based on an analysis of MEPS data on small firm employees, access rates, and enrollment, as well as IRS statistics of income (SOI) data, approximately 65 percent of eligible firms could use the credit at the time that health insurance benefit are provided to employees. We estimate that approximately 2.6 million of the 4.0 million firms estimated to be eligible for the credit would receive a current benefit from the tax credit in 2010.

The Federal small business health insurance tax credit provides a significant tax incentive to employers to offer health insurance to their employees. However, because the credit is nonrefundable, the credit will only provide a current incentive to those employers that have current Federal tax liability, however, it will be possible for businesses to carry any unused credit amount back one year and forward for up to 20 years.

VI. CONCLUSIONS

Individuals who lack health insurance coverage in the United States are more likely to work for a small employer as opposed to a large employer. There is a positive correlation between access to employer-provided health insurance and employer size (Table 13). On the other hand, at least 70 percent of employees with access to employer-provided health insurance elect to use it. Because the access rates increase with employer size, the participation rates (access rate multiplied by take-up rate) also increase with employer size.

The recession that began in December 2007 has had an adverse effect on employment-based health insurance coverage. As unemployment rates go up, the percentage of individuals with employment-based health insurance declines. From September 2007 to April 2009, employment-based health insurance coverage declined by 4.3 percent. However, the percentage decline was 10.7 percent for individuals employed by establishments with less than 25 employees, 6.9 percent for individuals employed by establishments with 25 to 99 employees, and 3.5 percent for individuals employed by establishments with at least 100 employees.[74]

Employment-based health insurance is the most common source of health insurance in the United States. Lack of access to employment-based health insurance among employees of small businesses has been one of the most intractable problems facing the U.S. health care system. While the Federal health care reform legislation enacted in 2010 does not mandate that employers offer health insurance to their employees, certain aspects of the legislation, such as the creation of health exchanges to which small businesses will have access and the adoption of a small business health insurance credit, are designed to encourage more small businesses to make health insurance available to their employees.

The states have tried a variety of approaches to improve health insurance coverage and, particularly, to improve the offering of health insurance by small businesses. However, we found that most state tax-incentive programs adopted apply to very narrow classes of employers (typically the smallest of employers) and provide relatively narrow tax benefits. In general, we found no correlation between any of these tax incentives and access rates for health insurance.

The Health Care Reform Act of 2010 adopted comprehensive changes to the U.S. health insurance system. The Act will set up state health exchanges that will offer individuals and small businesses access to health insurance, provide greater regulation of health insurance, and provide tax credits for individuals and small businesses to help offset the cost of health insurance.

The Health Care Reform Act affects small businesses in a variety of ways. Beginning in 2013, small businesses with 50 or more employees are assessed a $2,000 per worker fee if they do not provide health insurance to their employees and if any of their employees receive subsidized health insurance coverage through a health insurance exchange. In addition, beginning in 2014, small businesses with less than 100 employees will have access to health insurance through the state exchanges and, starting in 2017, the states will have the option of expanding the states' exchanges to businesses with more than 100 employees. In addition, employees of small businesses that do not offer health insurance will be able to purchase health insurance through the state exchanges.

One of the most significant aspects of health care reform for small businesses is the adoption of a generous tax credit to help subsidize the cost of small business health insurance. The credit is nonrefundable and generally is available only to offset current Federal income tax liability. Thus, employers who do not have sufficient current Federal income tax liability cannot immediately utilize the credit; unused credits can be carried back one year and carried forward 20 years.

A recent analysis estimated that approximately 4 million small businesses will be eligible for the small business health insurance tax credit nationwide and that approximately 1.2 million will be eligible for the full amount.[75] It is important to distinguish between eligibility for the credit and ability to apply the credit to current tax liabilities. Eligibility means that by virtue of the firm characteristics, the small business is eligible to claim the credit. Because the credit is nonrefundable, an employer can only use the credit immediately if the employer has positive Federal tax liability that the credit can offset.

Based on an analysis of MEPS data on small firm employees, access rates, and enrollment, as well as IRS statistics of income (SOI) data, approximately 65 percent of eligible firms could use the credit at the time that health insurance benefit are provided to employees. We estimate that approximately 2.6 million of the 4.0 million firms estimated to be eligible for the credit would receive a current benefit from the tax credit in 2010.

It remains to be seen whether the provisions in Federal health care reform will be sufficient to overcome the barriers to small businesses offering health insurance to their employees. While Federal health care reform will clearly overcome some of these barriers, the unpredictable costs associated with providing health insurance may continue to deter small businesses from offering health insurance to their employees. On the other hand, because Federal health care reform mandates that individuals have health insurance, demand for small businesses to offer health insurance should increase.

Table 13. Access, Take-Up, and Participation Rates, by Establishment Size, 2010 (Percent)

Firm Size, by Employment	Access	Take-up Rates	Participation
1 to 49	55	70	39
50 to 99	70	72	50
100 to 499	82	72	59
500 or more	88	78	68
Total: All Firms	71	73	51

Source: U.S. Bureau of Labor Statistics, National Compensation Survey, March 2010.

APPENDIX A. DATA ON HEALTH INSURANCE OFFERED BY SMALL BUSINESSES

Data in Table A1 show that 20 percent of eligible income tax returns claim the self-employed health insurance deduction. However, this utilization rate positively correlates with income and increases measurably for taxpayers with adjusted gross income of at least $100,000. Sole proprietors, partners, and S corporation shareholders may claim this deduction if they purchase health insurance in the individual market.

Tables A2 to A6 show the percent of establishments offering health insurance to employees, by firm size and by state.

Table A1. Percent of Individual Income Tax Returns that Claim the Self-Employed Health Insurance Deduction, 1998 to 2008, Percent of Returns and Percent of Returns by Adjusted Gross Income (AGI) Levels

	1998	1999	2000	2001	2002	2003	2004	2005	2006	2007	2008
Total Sole Prop Returns	20	20	20	20	19	20	19	19	18	17	16
No adjusted gross income	12	14	13	13	16	17	17	15	16	17	17
Under $10,000	09	10	11	10	10	11	10	10	7	7	8
$10,000 under $20,000	16	17	17	17	15	16	13	12	11	10	09
$20,000 under $30,000	20	21	20	19	20	19	19	17	17	15	16
$30,000 under $40,000	21	20	20	21	19	21	20	18	17	16	15
$40,000 under $50,000	18	19	19	20	18	19	19	17	17	18	16
$50,000 under $75,000	19	19	20	18	18	18	19	17	17	17	17
$75,000 under 100,000	21	21	19	19	19	21	20	21	18	18	16
$100,000 under $200,000	32	32	30	30	30	28	28	27	26	24	23
$200,000 under $500,000	53	53	52	54	55	52	53	52	48	48	46
$500,000 or more	81	79	79	88	93	90	85	83	81	81	84

Source: IRS, Statistics of Income, Table 1.4, Tax Years 1998 – 2008

Table A2. Percent of Private-Sector Establishments That Offer Health Insurance by State, 1998 to 2009‡

Firms with fewer than 10 employees

State	1998	1999	2000	2001	2002	2003	2004	2005	2006	2008	2009
United States	36	39	40	39	37	36	34	36	35	36	34
Alabama	30	46	41	31	40	36	39	38	40	40	34
Alaska				24		26	22	19	16	23	20
Arizona	33	36	44	38	28	29	33	34	27	27	31
Arkansas	23	23	23	23	†	20	20	16	24	20	23
California	35	39	39	39	38	37	34	41	38	40	37
Colorado	42	42	46	48	38	34	32	32	37	32	38
Connecticut	48	50	57	49	43	46	52	44	45	44	44
Delaware	40	†	†	49	31	42	43	33	38	38	38
District of Columbia	†	†	37	58	†	58	54	52	57	52	55
Florida	37	42	39	40	37	36	33	31	33	35	27
Georgia	34	32	30	30	29	29	30	28	25	31	30
Hawaii	†	84	†	69	83	75	69	81	82	80	76
Idaho	25	†	†	25	33	34	27	23	29	24	26
Illinois	38	40	38	41	39	31	35	31	31	34	31
Indiana	30	35	35	37	37	26	25	35	25	29	23
Iowa	31	31	30	31	28	27	26	26	31	33	28
Kansas	31	41	39	†	34	33	34	29	32	36	33
Kentucky	32	32	40	29	32	36	34	36	33	34	29
Louisiana	24	28	28	28	30	25	20	29	26	29	23
Maine	†	36	†	42	38	36	30	35	36	36	33
Maryland	40	51	37	38	37	37	44	42	48	37	42
Massachusetts	46	50	53	49	42	49	44	43	50	51	40
Michigan	40	50	45	51	45	42	39	43	33	36	33
Minnesota	37	35	34	43	35	31	34	32	27	29	36
Mississippi	00	27	30	22	26	25	19	21	21	21	21
Missouri	34	31	41	35	33	34	34	28	32	35	32
Montana	†	30	†	†	39	30	22	20	22	25	22
Nebraska	31	34	27	†	26	26	26	24	22	19	24
Nevada	†	38	†	36	24	37	30	31	40	44	30
New Hampshire	54	†	47	†	52	52	41	38	41	47	39
New Jersey	42	47	50	48	46	46	46	57	47	53	50
New Mexico	27	†	33	†	38	30	27	30	27	27	27
New York	43	45	48	47	40	44	42	44	45	43	44
North Carolina	36	33	38	32	25	34	33	37	36	30	24
North Dakota	†	†	31	†	†	28	27	31	27	33	30

Table A2. (Continued)

State	1998	1999	2000	2001	2002	2003	2004	2005	2006	2008	2009
Ohio	37	42	45	43	46	36	39	40	38	36	42
Oklahoma	26	32	29	31	33	26	20	25	32	30	24
Oregon	32	40	35	41	39	40	36	37	38	31	35
Pennsylvania	48	45	49	47	50	46	44	42	43	39	42
Rhode Island	†	52	†	44	†	48	44	41	49	46	43
South Carolina	29	35	38	26	25	32	30	30	25	29	28
South Dakota	†	†	25	†	†	26	26	29	20	26	29
Tennessee	23	32	31	30	26	26	26	27	30	32	29
Texas	27	33	30	26	27	26	20	26	26	26	28
Utah	43	†	27	32	30	27	30	21	27	31	24
Vermont	†	44	†	40		37	38	43	41	37	38
Virginia	37	39	39	38	39	40	39	34	38	36	28
Washington	36	39	41	36	38	38	37	36	33	41	34
West Virginia	34	†	32	†	34	26	26	21	25	29	25
Wisconsin	34	42	38	40	38	31	32	39	35	27	25
Wyoming	26	†	†	†	†	24	20	21	31	27	22
†States not shown separately	32	33	42	33	32						

‡ The MEPS did not release estimates for 2007.

† Survey data not collected for the year.

Source: Department of Health and Human Services, Medical Expenditure Panel Survey, various years.

Table A3. Percent of Private-Sector Establishments That Offer Health Insurance by State, 1998 to 2009‡
Firms with 10 to 24 employees

State	1998	1999	2000	2001	2002	2003	2004	2005	2006	2008	2009
United States	67	70	69	67	68	66	64	64	63	66	63
Alabama	71	63	77	74	66	72	70	65	69	78	58
Alaska	†	†	†	59		60	51	49	47	80	42
Arizona	60	66	64	57	61	66	53	46	36	79	38
Arkansas	58	62	64	49	†	44	61	44	38	74	43
California	59	68	63	61	64	59	62	67	65	77	62
Colorado	70	80	74	79	70	63	69	72	53	78	62
Connecticut	75	75	73	82	81	88	79	78	83	83	74
Delaware	74	†	†	70	73	65	69	69	63	73	68

State	1998	1999	2000	2001	2002	2003	2004	2005	2006	2008	2009
District of Columbia	†		63	78		90	81	82	77	75	74
Florida	63	61	68	64	61	66	57	63	61	62	67
Georgia	44	60	62	49	61	58	49	61	57	60	53
Hawaii	00	97	†	97	94	99	95	100	100	74	96
Idaho	55	†	†	52	†	64	51	54	58	77	53
Illinois	73	78	76	82	72	67	61	62	70	71	64
Indiana	63	63	71	64	60	61	59	54	58	68	43
Iowa	68	68	70	60	60	69	52	56	68	60	59
Kansas	62	68	71	†	59	66	58	63	62	71	62
Kentucky	71	69	83	71	75	67	70	59	70	68	66
Louisiana	58	55	47	62	58	56	42	53	47	61	52
Maine	†	61	†	46	64	66	71	76	73	68	76
Maryland	74	72	63	74	78	82	78	76	72	64	68
Massachusetts	79	79	83	83	80	81	71	77	75	70	76
Michigan	77	78	82	79	82	76	70	67	66	76	64
Minnesota	76	78	75	77	73	76	75	66	67	70	60
Mississippi	†	56	55	52	54	40	39	42	39	56	57
Missouri	71	71	56	52	63	65	59	65	68	62	67
Montana	†	56	†	†	56	62	50	55	63	61	57
Nebraska	48	65	65	†	51	56	53	46	46	62	50
Nevada	†	70	†	63	70	64	51	40	49	72	60
New Hampshire	71	†	83	†	74	86	77	83	78	60	76
New Jersey	79	82	76	85	69	68	81	82	69	73	77
New Mexico	55	†	53	†	62	60	48	60	56	60	55
New York	78	75	72	72	82	73	78	75	70	53	74
North Carolina	71	79	78	63	68	68	56	50	67	51	63
North Dakota	†	†	58	†	†	68	50	69	69	50	64
Ohio	71	74	71	82	74	62	70	72	71	62	72
Oklahoma	48	50	62	53	59	52	54	53	61	53	51
Oregon	72	65	75	69	70	69	70	71	75	50	54
Pennsylvania	75	76	89	71	75	80	78	70	73	61	66
Rhode Island	†	71	†	84	†	84	77	81	85	56	69
South Carolina	76	76	62	43	60	63	47	46	66	62	58
South Dakota	†	†	63	†	†	65	68	70	57	53	70
Tennessee	58	58	63	65	45	60	57	48	52	64	57
Texas	56	57	53	54	59	48	48	53	44	57	53
Utah	51	†	75	47	62	57	50	51	39	57	54
Vermont	†	81	†	81	†	78	61	62	70	56	82
Virginia	60	80	71	74	69	73	73	63	79	54	66
Washington	65	67	74	62	70	76	69	70	66	65	64

Table A3. (Continued)

State	1998	1999	2000	2001	2002	2003	2004	2005	2006	2008	2009
West Virginia	58	†	65	†	54	62	52	63	48	97	54
Wisconsin	82	77	71	76	73	77	71	70	53	66	61
Wyoming	55	†	†	†	61	55	59	38	54	62	53
†States not shown separately	66	69	69	68	59						

‡ The MEPS did not release estimates for 2007.
† Survey data not collected for the year.
Source: Department of Health and Human Services, Medical Expenditure Panel Survey, various years.

Table A4. Percent of private-sector establishments that offer health insurance by State, 1998 to 2009‡
Firms with 25 to 99 employees

State	1998	1999	2000	2001	2002	2003	2004	2005	2006	2008	2009
United States	84	85	85	83	82	81	81	83	82	81	82
Alabama	98	94	82	89	91	90	81	94	92	74	88
Alaska	†	†	†	75	†	75	77	74	77	80	64
Arizona	78	84	85	82	73	80	64	65	75	73	76
Arkansas	81	69	73	69	†	69	71	56	71	70	72
California	77	79	77	81	77	80	83	87	79	78	82
Colorado	85	82	85	90	77	85	81	88	88	81	84
Connecticut	91	85	94	92	98	85	93	98	96	91	92
Delaware	91	†	†	83	81	93	87	74	80	92	86
District of Columbia	†	†	89	83	†	93	90	87	91	91	87
Florida	69	85	85	75	85	78	72	80	72	85	79
Georgia	81	82	80	80	85	76	68	78	83	77	79
Hawaii	†	100	†	100	98	100	98	100	95	99	99
Idaho	80	†	†	77	†	83	85	76	65	85	75
Illinois	80	89	92	88	90	82	87	86	86	84	85
Indiana	86	80	86	80	85	73	84	83	75	83	79
Iowa	89	80	91	86	78	87	89	75	80	92	90
Kansas	85	82	91		68	83	83	86	83	77	86
Kentucky	88	88	85	92	85	82	79	82	76	82	86

State	1998	1999	2000	2001	2002	2003	2004	2005	2006	2008	2009
Louisiana	79	86	70	77	81	84	73	72	81	81	73
Maine	†	93	†	88	89	77	77	89	91	87	86
Maryland	88	89	89	94	87	88	88	87	86	84	84
Massachusetts	90	93	91	91	94	95	100	95	84	96	91
Michigan	91	92	88	87	87	74	86	78	90	71	85
Minnesota	86	95	81	76	84	80	83	91	89	84	75
Mississippi	†	72	72	72	77	69	72	81	68	79	78
Missouri	90	83	86	87	84	85	88	78	88	78	80
Montana	†	68	†	†	71	74	76	85	88	66	77
Nebraska	85	92	92	†	82	79	78	91	75	86	77
Nevada	†	91	†	76	89	85	77	83	73	79	75
New Hampshire	90	†	93	†	93	94	91	93	93	94	89
New Jersey	91	82	86	92	91	91	93	87	85	92	90
New Mexico	74	†	71	†	70	63	74	65	64	79	72
New York	85	85	91	91	87	89	85	87	85	85	90
North Carolina	90	90	82	83	79	79	73	84	89	82	76
North Dakota	†	†	89	†	†	80	79	78	86	90	91
Ohio	92	93	86	85	90	89	86	86	89	77	82
Oklahoma	83	82	80	79	70	69	81	84	82	73	77
Oregon	79	87	92	81	83	89	66	77	84	82	83
Pennsylvania	88	93	91	94	83	84	93	84	93	90	85
Rhode Island	†	92	†	93	†	89	86	92	86	90	96
South Carolina	78	82	84	85	69	82	66	81	69	82	78
South Dakota	†	†	74	†	†	80	78	85	72	76	81
Tennessee	86	82	84	84	82	70	83	82	73	78	86
Texas	81	71	76	63	70	65	64	68	65	71	68
Utah	74	†	83	86	89	78	78	75	75	71	73
Vermont	†	92	†	80	†	88	86	93	97	89	91
Virginia	85	85	86	91	76	87	97	85	87	85	81
Washington	91	93	85	80	79	80	79	63	90	88	84
West Virginia	68	†	91	†	80	76	75	78	69	77	77
Wisconsin	94	97	90	89	92	89	78	89	89	87	88
Wyoming	79	†	†	†	77	80	77	69	75	82	72
†States not shown separately	78	88	88	82	80						

‡ The MEPS did not release estimates for 2007.

† Survey data not collected for the year.

Source: Department of Health and Human Services, Medical Expenditure Panel Survey, various years

Table A5. Percent of private-sector establishments that offer health insurance by State, 1998 to 2009‡
Firms with 100 to 999 employees

State	1998	1999	2000	2001	2002	2003	2004	2005	2006	2008	2009
United States	**94**	**95**	**95**	**95**	**95**	**94**	**94**	**94**	**94**	**95**	**94**
Alabama	100	93	93	94	99	98	93	91	86	97	92
Alaska	†	†	†	97	†	96	100	97	95	99	94
Arizona	96	96	92	96	94	82	90	97	95	97	96
Arkansas	100	86	94	88	†	98	94	94	95	98	94
California	96	92	96	95	95	91	91	95	92	93	90
Colorado	96	90	100	95	96	79	93	97	92	96	92
Connecticut	97	100	96	100	100	99	100	98	100	94	97
Delaware	68	†	†	100	93	86	90	81	84	83	89
District of Columbia	†	†	82	98	†	100	100	97	93	95	100
Florida	97	96	96	97	89	94	99	96	100	92	94
Georgia	88	94	95	93	95	86	92	93	93	95	89
Hawaii	†	100	†	97	100	100	98	100	100	98	98
Idaho	98	†	†	93	†	95	98	91	100	87	95
Illinois	98	94	95	93	97	95	98	96	93	97	95
Indiana	97	96	97	96	98	95	98	92	95	96	94
Iowa	95	97	97	93	97	99	98	100	96	97	96
Kansas	93	94	90	†	91	95	95	92	94	96	92
Kentucky	91	91	95	98	92	99	97	87	93	94	95
Louisiana	86	97	91	89	95	89	99	90	94	95	90
Maine	†	97	†	100	99	99	93	99	100	100	99
Maryland	100	100	82	100	99	93	97	95	95	100	96
Massachusetts	94	98	95	99	95	89	100	91	92	99	99
Michigan	87	96	91	100	97	88	100	94	97	99	94
Minnesota	95	95	100	99	89	100	95	100	100	90	97
Mississippi	†	97	95	92	94	97	83	93	97	97	90
Missouri	92	96	96	97	97	82	92	95	95	100	98
Montana	†	99	†	†	98	95	93	88	100	97	97
Nebraska	98	98	99	†	99	91	91	97	95	97	95
Nevada	†	94	†	95	97	94	93	96	89	91	89
New Hampshire	95	†	100	†	100	100	100	92	92	99	98
New Jersey	90	99	96	94	94	92	92	94	100	99	99
New Mexico	93		92	†	91	93	92	94	86	88	92
New York	95	94	99	98	99	99	99	97	100	98	94
North Carolina	87	99	98	97	100	99	88	93	87	99	98

State	1998	1999	2000	2001	2002	2003	2004	2005	2006	2008	2009
North Dakota	†	†	82	†	†	98	92	92	92	91	94
Ohio	98	96	98	98	97	96	99	94	96	95	97
Oklahoma	93	91	96	99	92	94	93	95	90	93	94
Oregon	92	98	97	93	97	100	88	95	94	98	93
Pennsylvania	94	92	93	100	93	98	97	87	96	94	98
Rhode Island	†	97	†	98	†	100	100	100	100	99	96
South Carolina	97	93	94	91	94	93	92	96	86	97	95
South Dakota	†	†	98	†	†	90	99	99	93	97	98
Tennessee	97	96	94	96	96	95	100	97	100	99	93
Texas	90	94	90	88	92	94	84	91	84	89	91
Utah	96	†	96	96	99	96	83	93	86	88	94
Vermont	†	99	†	100	†	99	97	90	100	98	100
Virginia	88	97	89	99	100	92	99	99	99	100	98
Washington	91	97	100	91	95	97	98	98	94	100	97
West Virginia	94	†	95	†	93	98	87	87	88	91	91
Wisconsin	98	100	96	97	96	88	98	97	96	97	93
Wyoming	93	†	†	†	96	84	88	93	100	89	91
†States not shown separately	96	96	92	96	94						

‡ The MEPS did not release estimates for 2007.

† Survey data not collected for the year.

Source: Department of Health and Human Services, Medical Expenditure Panel Survey, various years

Table A6. Percent of Private-Sector Establishments That Offer Health Insurance by State, 1998 to 2009‡
Firms with 1,000 or more employees

State	1998	1999	2000	2001	2002	2003	2004	2005	2006	2008	2009
United States	99	99	99	99	99	99	99	99	98	99	99
Alabama	99	99	100	99	100	100	100	99	100	100	99
Alaska	†	†	†	99	†	100	98	97	96	98	99
Arizona	†	99	100	100	99	99	98	100	100	100	99
Arkansas	97	100	100	97	†	94	97	94	93	98	99
California	†	100	100	100	98	96	100	100	99	99	99
Colorado	†	100	100	100	94	100	98	100	97	100	100
Connecticut	99	100	97	100	100	97	97	99	99	100	100

Table A6. (Continued)

State	1998	1999	2000	2001	2002	2003	2004	2005	2006	2008	2009
Delaware	96	†	†	95	91	99	96	98	92	95	94
District of Columbia	†	†	99	98	†	100	99	97	100	99	100
Florida	100	100	99	99	100	100	97	98	99	99	98
Georgia	100	99	99	96	95	100	100	97	97	100	100
Hawaii	†	99	†	100	100	100	100	100	98	100	97
Idaho	†	†	†	98	†	100	100	100	93	100	100
Illinois	100	96	100	100	99	100	100	99	100	100	99
Indiana	93	100	99	100	100	100	100	97	100	100	100
Iowa	100	99	97	97	93	100	100	100	97	99	100
Kansas	99	100	99	†	100	100	98	100	98	100	99
Kentucky	98	100	99	100	100	89	98	100	100	99	99
Louisiana	97	100	100	100	100	100	97	98	98	100	100
Maine	†	100	†	100	100	99	100	100	96	100	99
Maryland	100	100	99	100	100	99	100	100	100	100	99
Massachusetts	99	100	99	100	100	100	100	100	100	100	100
Michigan	99	98	97	100	97	100	100	100	98	99	99
Minnesota	100	99	100	99	100	100	98	100	98	100	100
Mississippi	†	99	99	100	99	99	99	96	99	99	100
Missouri	100	100	100	99	100	97	100	100	99	98	99
Montana	†	100	†	†	91	96	95	95	100	97	100
Nebraska	95	97	96	†	99	100	100	98	98	100	100
Nevada	†	99	†	100	97	97	100	99	95	96	99
New Hampshire	100	†	97	†	93	100	100	100	97	100	100
New Jersey	100	100	100	99	100	97	100	96	100	100	100
New Mexico	†	†	98	†	91	100	96	97	100	98	99
New York	100	99	100	100	100	100	100	100	100	98	100
North Carolina	100	100	100	100	100	98	97	100	100	100	100
North Dakota	†	†	100	†	†	100	100	100	97	100	100
Ohio	100	100	100	100	99	100	99	99	98	100	100
Oklahoma	99	100	100	98	100	100	91	98	97	98	98
Oregon	†	100	100	98	100	100	100	100	96	100	99
Pennsylvania	100	100	99	100	100	100	100	100	98	99	100
Rhode Island	†	96	†	100	†	100	90	99	98	98	100
South Carolina	100	100	100	100	100	100	100	100	96	100	100
South Dakota	†	†	100	†	†	97	95	100	100	100	100

State	1998	1999	2000	2001	2002	2003	2004	2005	2006	2008	2009
Tennessee	100	100	100	99	100	98	100	99	97	98	99
Texas	100	97	99	100	100	99	99	98	98	95	98
Utah	†	†	100	100	90	98	92	100	98	99	100
Vermont	†	100	†	100	†	100	98	100	100	100	100
Virginia	98	98	99	100	100	97	98	98	98	100	100
Washington	†	100	95	99	99	100	99	98	98	97	100
West Virginia	100	†	100	†	100	100	97	100	97	100	100
Wisconsin	100	100	100	100	100	100	100	100	100	100	100
Wyoming	†	†	†	†	100	98	98	100	99	98	97
†States not shown separately	100	100	99	99	98						

‡ The MEPS did not release estimates for 2007.
† Survey data not collected for the year.
Source: Department of Health and Human Services, Medical Expenditure Panel
    Survey, various years

APPENDIX B. CURRENT FEDERAL TAX INCENTIVES FOR HEALTH INSURANCE

A. Overview

The Patient Protection and Affordable Care Act (PPACA), as amended by the Health Care and Education Reconciliation Act of 2010 (referred to as the "2010 Health Care Reform Act") modified the Federal tax incentives for health insurance and health benefits. These modified Federal tax incentives are taken into account for purposes of the analysis in the body of this paper. This section provides a brief overview of the modified Federal tax incentives.

Individuals who have employer-sponsored health insurance are eligible for more favorable tax treatment under Federal law than individuals who purchase health insurance on their own. The value of the employer-provided health insurance is excludable from income for income tax and employment tax purposes, which provides an incentive for employees to prefer to receive a portion of their wages in the form of employer-provided health insurance.

The 2010 Health Care Reform Act requires individuals to have health insurance coverage or to pay a penalty based on household income beginning in 2014. Individuals who do not have access to employer-sponsored health insurance will be able to purchase health insurance coverage through a state health insurance exchange. Low- and moderate-income individuals and families who purchase health insurance through an exchange will be entitled to tax credits to help offset the costs of the health insurance coverage.

The 2010 Health Care Reform Act does not include a so-called "mandate" that employers offer health insurance coverage to their employees. However, employers with at least 50 full-time equivalent (FTE) employees that do not offer health insurance coverage to their employees will be required to pay a penalty with respect to any full-time employees who purchase health insurance through an exchange and who are entitled to a tax-credit or cost-sharing subsidy for that insurance. In addition, beginning in 2014, employers who offer health insurance coverage will be charged the penalty with respect to employees who purchase health insurance through a state exchange if the employee is eligible for a tax credit or cost-sharing subsidy.

B. Tax Provisions Relating to Individuals Who Purchase Health Insurance on Their Own

1. Itemized Deduction for Out-of-Pocket Medical Expenses (IRC Sec. 213)[76]

Historically, individual taxpayers who itemize their deductions have been entitled to deduct their out-of-pocket medical expenses to the extent that these expenses exceed a threshold. Prior to the enactment of the 2010 Health Care Reform Act, the threshold for the medical expense deduction was 7.5 percent of adjusted gross income (AGI). Under the 2010 Health Care Reform Act, beginning in 2013, the threshold for the itemized deduction for medical expenses is increased to 10 percent of AGI, except that the 7.5 percent of AGI threshold applies until 2017 for individuals who are age 65 and older.

The itemized deduction for individuals for medical expenses benefits fewer individuals than the Federal tax benefits applicable to employment-based health insurance. First, the deduction is only available to those taxpayers who itemize their deductions. Further, the deduction is only available if the medical expenses exceed a relatively high percentage of AGI. Thus, for example, in 2008, 48.8 million taxpayers filed Schedule A (itemized deductions) with their Federal income tax return and, of those, 10.1 million included amounts for medical and dental expenses.

2. Tax Credits for the Purchase of Health Insurance (new IRC Sec. 36B)

Effective in 2014, the 2010 Health Care Reform provides a tax credit for qualifying taxpayers who purchase health insurance through a health insurance exchange. This credit – the premium assistance credit – is refundable and payable in advance directly to the insurer. Taxpayers are eligible for the credit if their household income is between 100 percent and 400 percent of the Federal poverty level. The credit design limits the percentage of premiums that low- and moderate-income taxpayers are required to pay for health insurance coverage through the exchange. This percentage ranges from 2 percent for the taxpayers at 100 percent of the Federal poverty level to 9.5 percent for taxpayers at 400 percent of the Federal poverty level.

3. Health Care Tax Credit (HCTC) (IRC Sec. 35)

Certain displaced workers (i.e., workers who are receiving trade adjustment assistance payments) and certain workers receiving pension benefits from the Pension Benefit Guaranty Corporation (PBGC) are entitled to a refundable tax credit if they purchase continuation health insurance coverage under COBRA, purchase certain state-based coverage, or purchase certain other health insurance coverage. The credit equals 80 percent (65 percent for years before 2011) of the amount paid for health insurance coverage. This credit is available to a relatively narrow class of taxpayers.

C. Exclusion from Income for Employer-Sponsored Health Insurance (IRC Sections 104, 105, 106, 125, 3121(a), and 3306(a))

One of the reasons that employment-based health insurance became a prominent form of health insurance in the United States is the exclusion from income for employees of the value of employer-provided care that they receive. If an employer contributes to a plan to provide health coverage to employees (through health insurance or through a self-funded health plan), the employer contributions and the amount of any benefits that an employee receives from the plan are not included in the employee's income for Federal income and payroll tax purposes. There is no dollar limit on the amount of employer-provided health care that is excludable from income.

Employers are entitled to deduct the amounts they contribute for employee health care, just as they are entitled to deduct cash compensation paid and other allowable benefits to employees. Thus, from a Federal income tax perspective, employers are indifferent as to whether they pay compensation in cash or in the form of health care because both payments are deductible by the employer. The value of employer-provided health insurance is also excluded from wages for employment tax purposes, lowering both the employer and employer share of employment taxes that must be paid.

Employers may also maintain a cafeteria plan, which typically offers employees a choice between cash compensation and certain nontaxable benefits. If the cafeteria plan satisfies certain requirements, then amounts received as nontaxable benefits are excluded from an employee's income for income and payroll tax purposes.[77] One of the benefits that a cafeteria plan might provide is the opportunity for an employee to forego current compensation in order to pay for the employee's share of health insurance premiums.[78] This allows the employee to convert what otherwise would be taxable wages (the employee's share of health insurance premiums) into a nontaxable benefit.

D. Deduction for Health Insurance Premiums of Self-Employed Individuals (IRC sec. 162(l))

Self-employed individuals are entitled to a deduction from their income for Federal income tax (but not employment tax) purposes for the health insurance costs of the self-employed individual and his or her spouse and dependents. The amount of this deduction cannot exceed the amount of the individual's self-employment income. Self-employed individuals include sole proprietors, partners in partnerships, and more than two percent shareholders in S corporations.

Because the deduction for health insurance premiums of self-employed individuals does not apply for employment tax purposes, the treatment of self-employed individuals for Federal tax purposes is less favorable than the treatment of employees, who are entitled to exclude the value of health insurance benefits for income and employment tax purposes.

E. Flexible Spending Accounts and Health Reimbursement Arrangements (IRC sec. 125(i)

Employers may offer employees the opportunity to participate in a plan that reimburses employees for medical expenses not covered by health insurance. These arrangements include flexible spending accounts (FSAs) and health reimbursement arrangements (HRAs).

Under a typical FSA offered as part of a cafeteria plan, an employee foregoes a portion of their salary and that amount is credited to an FSA for the employee. Thus, the employee reduces his or her current cash compensation in order to have that amount available to reimburse the employee for out-of-pocket medical expenses. The advantage of using the FSA for the employee is that amounts credited to the FSA are not included in the employee's income for Federal income or employment tax purposes. In essence, an FSA allows an employee to avoid income and employment taxes on the amounts that they would have expended in any event for out-of-pocket medical expenses. However, if any amounts are remaining in an FSA at the end of a year, those amounts are forfeited (use it or lose it); thus, employees need to estimate their out-of-pocket medical expenses carefully to make sure they do not contribute too much to an FSA.

Current law does not limit the amounts that employees can contribute to an FSA each year. Under the PPACA, the amount that employees can set aside each year into an FSA is limited to $2,500, beginning in 2013.[79] This dollar limitation will be indexed for inflation after 2013.

Health reimbursement arrangements are similar to FSAs, except that funding is not on a salary reduction basis. Thus, an employer would make contributions of all (or a class of) employees and they can withdraw amounts to pay for out-of-pocket medical expenses. The use it or lose it rule does not apply to health reimbursement accounts. In addition, funds from the HSA may cover the employee share of the health insurance costs, but funds from a health FSA cannot.

F. Health Savings Accounts and Archer Medical Savings Accounts (IRC sec. 125(d)(2))

Special tax incentives encourage individuals to enroll in high deductible health plans. Under these rules, individuals may make tax-deductible contributions to a Health Savings Account (HSA), which is a tax-exempt account similar to an individual retirement arrangement (IRA).[80] The earnings on amounts contributed to an HSA are not subject to Federal income tax and withdrawals used for qualified medical expenses are not included in the individual's income. If an employer contributes to an employee's HSA, the contributions are excluded from the employee's income for Federal income and employment tax purposes.[81] In addition, employees may make HSA contributions through a cafeteria plan maintained by an employer.

A high deductible health plan must have an annual deductible that is at least $1,200 for self-only coverage or $2,400 for family coverage.[82] The sum of the deductible plus other out of pocket expenses cannot exceed $5,950 for self-only coverage and $11,900 for family coverage. The maximum annual contribution amount to an HSA is $3,050 for self-only coverage and $6,150 for family coverage; these amounts increase by $1,000 for each individual over age 55.

Archer Medical Savings Accounts (Archer MSA) are similar to, but less generous than, HSAs. Archer MSAs are only available to self-employed individuals and employees of small businesses. In addition, after 2007, the ability to contribute to Archer MSAs is limited to individuals who previously made Archer MSA contributions and employees covered under a high deductible health plan of an employer who previously participated in Archer MSAs.

G. Retiree Medical Benefits (IRC sec. 401(h), 419, 419A, and 501(c)(9))

Providing employees with health insurance coverage after retirement is a benefit primarily provided by large employers and, over time, fewer large employers are offering this retirement benefit. Under current law, employers can prefund, on a deductible basis, the costs attributable to retiree medical expenses over the working lives of the covered employees. Employers may contribute to a tax-exempt voluntary employees' beneficiary association (VEBA) or to a tax-qualified pension plan maintained by the employer (into a retiree medical account). In addition, if an employer maintains a qualified defined benefit pension plan with a retiree medical account, transfers of excess assets under the pension plan may fund the retiree medical account.

H. Small Business Health Insurance Tax Credit (IRC sec. 36B)

Under the Health Care Reform Act, certain small employers are eligible to claim a tax credit for contributions for employee health insurance. The credit is effective for years beginning after December 31, 2009. To be eligible for the credit, an employer must (1) pay at least 50 percent of the premiums for their employees' health insurance and (2) have less than 25 full-time equivalent (FTE) employees with average wages of less than $50,000.

Small businesses may use the small business health insurance non-refundable tax credit to offset Federal income tax liability. If the employer does not have sufficient tax liability to utilize the credit fully, the employer may carry the unused credit back one year and forward up to 20 years. Tax-exempt small businesses can use the credit to offset certain payroll taxes, which for this purpose includes amounts required to be withheld from employees' pay for Federal income tax purposes plus the employer and employer share of Medicare (i.e., HI) taxes.

The maximum credit rate is 35 percent of the employer contributions for health insurance for 2010-2013 and 50 percent of the employer contributions beginning in 2014. The maximum credit is available for employers with up to 10 FTE employees and average wages of up to $25,000. After that level, the credit rate phases down as the number of employees and average wages increases. Tables B1 and B2 show the phase down of the credit for 2010-2013 and for 2014 and thereafter.

Table B1. Maximum Small Business Health Insurance Tax Credit (Percentage of Employer Contribution to Premiums) 2010-2013[83]

Firm Size, by employment (FTEs)	Average Wage					
	Up to $25,000	$30,000	$35,000	$40,000	$45,000	$50,000
Up to 10	35	28	21	14	7	0
11	33	26	19	12	5	0
12	30	23	16	9	2	0
13	28	21	14	7	0	0
14	26	19	12	5	0	0
15	23	16	9	2	0	0
16	21	14	7	0	0	0
17	19	12	5	0	0	0
18	16	9	2	0	0	0
19	14	7	0	0	0	0
20	12	5	0	0	0	0
21	9	2	0	0	0	0
22	7	0	0	0	0	0
23	5	0	0	0	0	0
24	2	0	0	0	0	0
25	0	0	0	0	0	0

Source: Congressional Research Service, 2010.

**Table B2. Small Business Health Insurance Tax Credit
(Percentage of Employer Contribution to Premiums)
2014 and Subsequent Years**

Firm Size, by employment (FTEs)	Average Wage					
	Up to $25,000	$30,000	$35,000	$40,000	$45,000	$50,000
Up to 10	50	40	30	20	10	0
11	47	37	27	17	7	0
12	43	33	23	13	3	0
13	40	30	20	10	0	0
14	37	27	17	7	0	0
15	33	23	13	3	0	0
16	30	20	10	0	0	0
17	27	17	7	0	0	0
18	23	13	3	0	0	0
19	20	10	0	0	0	0
20	17	7	0	0	0	0
21	13	3	0	0	0	0
22	10	0	0	0	0	0
23	7	0	0	0	0	0
24	3	0	0	0	0	0
25	0	0	0	0	0	0

Source: Congressional Research Service, 2010.

I. Small Business Simple Cafeteria Plan (IRC sec. 125(j))

The Health Care Reform Act created a "simple cafeteria plan" for small employers. A small employer who maintains a simple cafeteria plan is not subject to certain nondiscrimination rules that otherwise would apply. For purposes of these rules, a small employer is defined as an employer with 100 or fewer employees. Under a simple cafeteria plan, an employer must make contributions on behalf of qualified employees equal to (1) a uniform percentage (not less than two percent) of each employee's compensation or (2) an amount not less than the lesser of six percent of employee compensation or two times the salary reduction contributions of each qualified employee. Qualified employees are nonhighly compensated employees who are not key employees who are eligible to participate in the plan.

APPENDIX C. SUMMARY OF STATE TAX PROVISIONS RELATING TO HEALTH INSURANCE

In addition to the Federal tax incentives that cause employees to prefer to receive health insurance through an employer-sponsored plan, state tax incentives may influence the preference for employer-sponsored health insurance. Every state with an income tax system allows self-employed individuals to claim the self-employed health insurance deduction against their income for state income tax purposes.[84] These states also provide an exclusion from income for employer-provided health insurance.

In a limited number of cases, states have adopted special small business tax incentives designed to encourage small businesses to offer health insurance coverage to their employees. Some states have adopted nontax programs designed to encourage or make it easier for small businesses to offer health insurance to their employees or to make it easier for employees of small businesses to purchase health insurance.

This section details the provisions enacted at the state level in four categories: (1) general health tax incentives, (2) provisions designed to encourage or require the use of cafeteria plans to offer health insurance, (3) specific provisions relating to small business tax incentives to offer health insurance, and (4) other provisions relating to small business health insurance. If a state does not have all four categories outlined, it means that there are no specific state law provisions in the omitted categories. In general, the rules outlined in this section were in effect on January 1, 2010; thus, this summary does not reflect any changes adopted subsequent to that date. Further, this section will not reflect any changes to state law that may be (or may have been) enacted in response to the enactment of Federal health care reform legislation.

Alabama

General Health Tax Incentives
Alabama allows a deduction for self-employed health insurance expenses and an exclusion for employer-provided health insurance for state income tax purposes.

Alabama allows an individual to claim an itemized deduction for medical and dental expenses (not including health insurance premiums paid by an employer-sponsored plan (cafeteria plan)) that exceed 4 percent of adjusted gross income.

Small Business Tax Incentives

Alabama permits businesses with fewer than 25 employees to deduct 150 percent of the amount they pay for employee health insurance premiums for state income tax purposes. Employees of businesses with fewer than 25 employees may claim a 50 percent deduction against their personal state income tax for amounts they pay as health insurance premiums as part of an employer-provided health insurance plan. To be eligible, employees must make $50,000 or less in annual wages and report no more than $75,000 in adjusted annual gross income ($150,000 in the case of a married couple filing a joint return). This provision was enacted in 2007 and became effective January 1, 2009.

Alaska

General Health Tax Incentives

Alaska allows corporations to deduct health insurance premiums paid on behalf of employees as a compensation expense. Alaska does not have an individual income tax, so there are no specific tax incentives provided for self-employed individuals and employees.

Arizona

General Health Tax Incentives

Arizona allows a deduction for self-employed health insurance expenses and an exclusion for employer-provided health insurance for state income tax purposes. In addition, Arizona generally follows the Medical Savings Account provisions of sec. 220 of the Internal Revenue Code. However, Arizona residents are permitted to set up MSAs in two situations in which they are not permitted under Federal law. A person can set up an MSA even though his or her employer is not a small employer (with 50 or fewer employees) and even if the maximum number of MSAs that can be set up under Federal law (750,000) has been reached.

Small Business Tax Incentives

Arizona allows a credit against premium tax liability incurred by a health care insurer that provides health insurance to individuals or small businesses certified by the Arizona Department of Revenue. Health insurance must be provided within 90 days after a certificate of eligibility is provided. For health insurance coverage issued to small businesses, the amount of the tax credit allowed is the lesser of $1,000 for coverage of a single person or $3,000 for family coverage; or 50 percent of the health insurance premium. The maximum amount of tax credits allowed to all taxpayers is capped at $5 million per calendar year. Eligible small businesses must have been in existence for at least one calendar year, not provided health insurance to its employees for at least six months, and had between 2 and 25 employees during the most recent calendar year.

Arkansas

General Health Tax Incentives

Arkansas allows a deduction for self-employed health insurance expenses and an exclusion for employer-provided health insurance for state income tax purposes.

In addition, Arkansas adopted Internal Revenue Code Sec. 106 concerning employer contributions to an employee Medical Savings Plan and IRC Sec. 138 concerning excluding Medicare plus MSA payments from income.

Arkansas also provides incentives for Health Savings Accounts (HSAs), which enable workers with high deductible health insurance to make pre-tax contributions equal to the lesser of the annual deductible or $3,000 for self-coverage ($5,950 for families) for 2009 to cover health care costs.

Other State Health Incentives

ARHealthNet (formerly called the Arkansas Safety Net Benefit Program) is a group health insurance program for small to medium size businesses (two to 500 employees) that have not offered health insurance for 12 months. This is a limited benefit plan with premiums subsidized for employees under 200 percent of the Federal poverty level. The program has employee participation requirements. Spouses who do not have health insurance are also eligible.

California

General Health Tax Incentives
California allows a deduction for self-employed health insurance expenses and exclusion for employer-provided health insurance for state income tax purposes.

Colorado

General Health Tax Incentives
Colorado allows a deduction for self-employed health insurance expenses and exclusion for employer-provided health insurance for state income tax purposes. In addition, Colorado permits employers (without regard to size) to establish Medical Savings Accounts for employees. The maximum amount that may be contributed on a tax-free basis on behalf of an employee is $3,000 per year.

For tax years during which the state's fiscal year ends with a qualified surplus, eligible resident individuals can claim a Colorado income tax credit for certain health benefit plan premiums that they pay for themselves, their spouses, or their dependents. The credit is up to $500 for certain low-income individuals. The health benefit plan credit was not available for tax years 2002 through 2010.

Connecticut

General Health Tax Incentives
Connecticut allows a deduction for self-employed health insurance expenses and exclusion for employer-provided health insurance for state income tax purposes.

State's Use of Cafeteria Plans to Provide Health Insurance
Connecticut requires any employer providing health insurance benefits paid partly through payroll deductions to offer a cafeteria plan, effective October 1, 2007.

Delaware

Delaware allows a deduction for self-employed health insurance expenses and exclusion for employer-provided health insurance for state income tax purposes.

District of Columbia

General Health Tax Incentives
The District of Columbia allows a deduction for self-employed health insurance expenses and an exclusion for employer-provided health insurance for state income tax purposes.

Florida

State's Use of Cafeteria Plans to Provide Health Insurance
The Cover Florida Health Care Access Program, enacted in May 2008, requires that employers who voluntarily choose to participate in the program comply with certain requirements, including establishing a cafeteria plan, Flexible Spending Arrangement or both.

Georgia

General Health Tax Incentives
Georgia allows a deduction for self-employed health insurance expenses and exclusion for employer-provided health insurance for state income tax

purposes. Georgia provides tax incentives to encourage high deductible health plans (HDHPs). Individuals are permitted to deduct premium costs paid for HDHPs. In addition, Georgia provides a specific tax incentive related to HDHPs for small businesses.

Small Business Tax Incentives

Georgia provides a nonrefundable tax credit for small employer high-deductible health plans up to $250 per year per enrolled employee. The credit is available for employers with 1 to 50 employees that make a HDHP available to employees. Employees must be enrolled in the plan for 12 consecutive months. The tax credit was effective beginning in 2009.

Hawaii

General Health Tax Incentives

Hawaii allows a deduction for self-employed health insurance expenses and exclusion for employer-provided health insurance for state income tax purposes.

Other State Health Provisions

The Hawaii Prepaid Health Care Act requires all Hawaii businesses to provide health insurance to employees who work at least 20 hours per week for four consecutive weeks.[85]

Idaho

General Health Tax Incentives

Idaho allows a deduction for self-employed health insurance expenses and exclusion for employer-provided health insurance for state income tax purposes.

Small Business Tax Incentives

Idaho provides a credit for employer-provided health insurance. The credit is available for any taxable year during which the number of new employees increases above the average employment of the firm in prior years. A $1,000 credit is permitted for each new employee who, in the calendar year ending during the taxable year for which the credit is claimed, received annual earnings at an average rate of $15.50 or more per hour and was eligible for employer-provided accident or health coverage. A $500 credit is permitted per new employee who does not meet the $1,000 criteria, but who is employed in a revenue-producing enterprise.

The total credit allowed cannot exceed 3.25 percent of net income from the taxpayer's revenue-producing enterprise in which the employment occurred. The amount of this and all other permissible tax credits cannot exceed 50 percent of the taxpayer's tax liability. Any tax credit can be carried over to the three succeeding taxable years.

Illinois

General Health Tax Incentives
Illinois allows a deduction for self-employed health insurance expenses and exclusion for employer-provided health insurance for state income tax purposes. In addition, Illinois adopted Medical Savings Account provisions similar to Federal law.

Indiana

General Health Tax Incentives
Indiana allows a deduction for self-employed health insurance expenses and exclusion for employer-provided health insurance for state income tax purposes. In addition, Indiana allows a deduction for contributions to Health Savings Accounts, and contributions to Archer MSAs for state individual income tax purposes.

Indiana provides a tax credit for new employer-provided health insurance, effective January 1, 2007. The credit is available to pass-through entities such as partnerships and S corporations. The credit applies to section 125 cafeteria plans. The credit is the lesser of $50 per enrolled employee per year or $2,500 for two years. The employer must not have provided insurance for one year prior to claiming the credit and must offer insurance to eligible employees (those who work at least 30 hours per week) and their dependents. This credit was effective January 2008.

Small Business Tax Incentives

Indiana provides a small employer wellness tax credit program. The credit is available to S corporations and partnerships. This credit allows employers with 2 to 100 employees to claim a tax credit for 50 percent of the costs incurred in a given year for providing qualified wellness programs to their employees. This provision was enacted in 2007.

Iowa

General Health Tax Incentives

Iowa allows an exclusion for employer-provided health insurance for state income tax purposes. In addition, Iowa allows individuals (including self-employed individuals) to deduct 100 percent of the amount paid for health and dental insurance premiums. The deduction is not available with respect to health insurance premiums paid on a pretax basis. Iowa allows taxpayers to claim the Health Savings Account deduction from their Federal individual income tax return.

State's Use of Cafeteria Plans to Provide Health Insurance

Iowa enacted a law in 2008 that requires the Commissioner of Insurance to assist employers with 25 or fewer employees to implement and administer a cafeteria plan including medical expense reimbursement accounts. The law also mandates a study of the ramifications of requiring employers with at least 10 employees to adopt and maintain a cafeteria plan.

Kansas

General Health Tax Incentives

Kansas allows a deduction for self-employed health insurance expenses and exclusion for employer-provided health insurance for state income tax purposes. It also allows a deduction for contributions to Health Savings Account deduction for individual income tax purposes.

State's Use of Cafeteria Plans to Provide Health Insurance

Kansas passed a law in 2008 requiring all insurers to offer premium-only cafeteria plans. In 2007, Kansas appropriated $150,000 toward a small employer cafeteria plan development fund.

Small Business Tax Incentives

Kansas provides a refundable small employer health insurance credit. The employer must have established a small employer health benefit plan or made contributions to a Health Savings Account of an eligible employee after December 31, 2004. The employer must not have contributed within the 2 years prior to claiming the credit to any health insurance premium or Health Savings Account on behalf of an eligible employee. Eligible employees must work at least 30 hours per week. The credit equals $70 per month per enrolled employee; the credit amount decreases for each year of the credit ($70, $50, $35) for a maximum of three years.

For employers that established a small employer health benefit plan after December 1, 1999, and before January 1, 2005, the amount of the credit was $35 per month per eligible covered employee or 50 percent of the total paid by the employer during the tax year, whichever is less, for the first two years of participation. The credit decreases to 75 percent of this amount in the third year, 50 percent in the fourth year, and 25 percent in the fifth year. No credit is allowed after the fifth year. Taxpayers claiming the credit must reduce the amount of the deduction for related expenses by the amount of the credit.

Kentucky

General Health Tax Incentives

Kentucky allows an exclusion for employer-provided health insurance for state income tax purposes. Kentucky allows individuals, including self-employed individuals, to deduct from gross income 100 percent of medical and dental insurance premiums paid with after-tax dollars.

Other State Health Incentives

The Insurance Coverage, Affordability and Relief to Employers (ICARE) program provides a subsidy (decreasing for each year in the program) of $40 to $60 per employee per month to small businesses that pay at least 50 percent of the premium for health insurance, have been uninsured for at least 12 months, and have average employee wages below 300 percent of the Federal poverty level. A small business is one with two to 25 employees.

Louisiana

General Health Tax Incentives

Louisiana allows a deduction for self-employed health insurance expenses and exclusion for employer-provided health insurance for state income tax purposes.

Maine

General Health Tax Incentives

Maine allows a deduction for self-employed health insurance expenses and exclusion for employer-provided health insurance for state income tax purposes.

Small Business Tax Incentives

Maine provides a tax credit for small employer health plans. The credit was the lesser of 20 percent of dependent health benefits paid or $125 per year per enrolled low-income employee with dependent coverage. Credit may not exceed 50 percent of the state income liability. The employer can claim the credit for low-income employees who work at least 30 hours per week or 1,000 hours per year. The employer must provide health insurance for dependents of low-income employees. The employer must have no more than five employees and meet contribution requirements. There is no duration limit; the credit is nonrefundable. The credit was implemented in 2001.

Other State Health Incentives

Maine's DirigoChoice covers small businesses with two to 50 employees, self-employed individuals, and other individuals. Small business employers and self-employed individuals must contribute 60 percent of the cost of health insurance premiums to be eligible for the premium assistance subsidy. DirigoChoice is currently open only for small employers.

Maryland

General Health Tax Incentives
Maryland allows a deduction for self-employed health insurance expenses and exclusion for employer-provided health insurance for state income tax purposes. In addition, Maryland excludes contributions to Health Savings Account from income for purposes of the individual income tax.

Other State Health Incentives
The Working Families and Small Business Health Coverage Act offers subsidies to small businesses with two to nine employees and an average wage below $50,000 of up to 50 percent of the premium cost for health insurance. The maximum subsidy per employee depends on the health insurance coverage chosen and the average annual wage for the business. Any planned employer contribution to an employee's Health Savings Account is treated as an additional employer premium contribution in calculating the premium subsidy. The employer cannot have offered health insurance to employees in the previous 12 months. This program took effect October 1, 2008. The subsidy is shared between the employer and each employee based on the share of the premium that each contributes. Those employers that join are required to offer a cafeteria plan to their employees. Enrollment in the program is capped to stay within a budget of $15 million.

Massachusetts

General Health Tax Incentives
Massachusetts allows an exclusion for employer-provided health insurance for state income tax purposes and a deduction for self-employed health insurance. The Massachusetts Health Care Reform Act requires most adults age 18 and over with access to affordable health insurance to purchase it. If an individual fails to comply with this requirement, the penalties are imposed on the individual's personal income tax return and shall not exceed 50 percent of the minimum monthly insurance premium for which an individual would have qualified. The penalties only apply to adults who are deemed able to afford health insurance.

State's Use of Cafeteria Plans to Provide Health Insurance

Beginning in 2007, Massachusetts became the first state to require all employers with 11 or more employees to offer at least a premium-only cafeteria plan. This provision was one of the primary employer responsibilities in a larger universal health plan. Employers must make a "fair and reasonable" contribution toward an employee health plan or pay a state assessment of up to $295 per employee, per year.

Other State Health Incentives

The Insurance Partnerships in Massachusetts offers premium assistance for small businesses with two to 50 employees that have not offered health insurance in the past six months, will have an employer contribution toward the premiums of at least 50 percent, and have at least one employee who earns below 300 percent of the Federal poverty level.

Michigan

General Health Tax Incentives

Michigan allows a deduction for self-employed health insurance expenses and exclusion for employer-provided health insurance for state income tax purposes.

Minnesota

General Health Tax Incentives

Minnesota allows a deduction for self-employed health insurance expenses and exclusion for employer-provided health insurance for state income tax purposes.

A nonrefundable credit is provided equal to 20 percent of the health insurance premiums paid during the first 12 months of participation in a cafeteria plan for health care. This credit is allowed only for individuals who did not have health care coverage for the previous 12 months and whose household income falls below the eligible range.

State's Use of Cafeteria Plans to Provide Health Insurance

Effective July 2009, Minnesota requires employers with 11 or more employees who do not offer health insurance to establish a cafeteria plan. The employer is not required to establish a health plan or contribute to the cafeteria plan and employees can opt out of participation. Employers may "opt out" of this requirement by certifying to the Commissioner of Commerce that they have received education and information on the advantages of cafeteria plans and have chosen not to establish such a plan.

Other State Health Incentives

Minnesota offers grants of up to $350 to certain small employers (with 2 to 50 employees) that establish cafeteria plans to help offset the costs of setting up the plan.

Mississippi

General Health Tax Incentives

Mississippi allows a deduction for self-employed health insurance expenses and exclusion for employer-provided health insurance for state income tax purposes. In addition, Mississippi allows a deduction for contributions to Health Savings Accounts.

Missouri

General Health Tax Incentives

Missouri allows a deduction for self-employed health insurance expenses and exclusion for employer-provided health insurance for state income tax purposes.

State's Use of Cafeteria Plans to Provide Health Insurance

Effective January 1, 2008, Missouri requires all employers with health insurance plans (other than self-insured plans) and that pay a portion of the premiums to offer a cafeteria plan to employees.

Small Business Tax Incentives

Missouri provides a self-employed health insurance tax credit. Effective August 28, 2007, a self-employed taxpayer who is otherwise ineligible for the health insurance deduction allowed under IRC section 162 is allowed a personal income tax credit for the federal tax paid on amounts that the taxpayer has paid for self-employed health insurance. The credit allowed is equal to the portion of the taxpayer's federal tax liability incurred as a result of the taxpayer's inclusion of such amounts in federal adjusted gross income. To the extent that the allowable credit exceeds the taxpayer's state income tax liability, the excess will be considered an overpayment of tax and will be refunded. The credit is not transferable.

Montana

General Health Tax Incentives

Montana allows a deduction for self-employed health insurance expenses and exclusion for employer-provided health insurance for state income tax purposes. Montana also allows a deduction for contributions to Health Savings Accounts for state tax purposes. Shareholders in S corporations are allowed to deduct the cost of health insurance premiums for state tax purposes.

Montana provides an exemption from state income tax for deposits made into a Montana Medical Savings Account. Annual exclusion from gross income is permitted for up to $3,000 of contributions plus accumulated interest and other earnings. For married couple filing a joint return, exclusion is $3,000 per spouse.

Small Business Tax Incentives

Montana provides a nonrefundable credit for small business employers (Health Insurance for Uninsured Montanans Credit). To qualify for this credit, the employer must have been in business in Montana for at least 12 months, must employ 20 or fewer employees who work at least 20 hours per week, and must pay at least 50 percent of each Montana employee's insurance premium. The credit is only available for three years. The tax credit is limited to a maximum of 10 employees and equals 50 percent of the percentage of employer premiums paid times $25 per month per covered employee.

A separate credit is also available (Insure Montana Small Business Health Insurance Credit). Beginning in 2006, a refundable tax credit is available against corporation license (income) tax as part of a program established to provide small businesses with assistance in paying for group health insurance. An eligible employer that does not receive premium assistance payments or premium incentive payments through the small business health insurance pool may claim a credit of not more than $100 each month for each employee and $100 each month for each employee's spouse (if the employer covers the spouse), if the average age of the group is 45 years of age or older; and not more than $40 each month for each covered dependent, not to exceed two dependents of an employee in addition to the employee's spouse. An employer may not claim a credit in excess of 50 percent of the total premiums paid by the employer for the qualifying small groups, for premiums paid from a Medical Savings Account, or for premiums for which a deduction is claimed in computing corporation license or personal income tax. If an eligible employer's tax credit exceeds the employer's corporation license or personal income tax liability, the excess amount must be refunded. Eligible small employers proposing to apply for a tax credit must be registered each year with the Commissioner.

As of January 2009, both the small business tax credit and the purchasing pool programs were at full capacity because of limited funding. Small businesses applying for either program are being put on a waiting list. The program is funded through increases in Montana's tobacco tax.

Other State Health Incentives

Beginning in 2005, Insure Montana offers assistance to small businesses with two to nine employees currently not offering insurance. These businesses can receive monthly assistance payments amounting to roughly $100 per employee for both the employer's and the employee's portion of the health insurance premium. To be eligible, the business can have no employee who earns more than $75,000, other than the owner of the business.

Nebraska

General Health Tax Incentives

Nebraska allows a deduction for self-employed health insurance expenses and exclusion for employer-provided health insurance for state income tax purposes. Nebraska also allows a deduction for contributions to Health Savings Accounts for state tax purposes.

Nevada

Other State Health Incentives

Nevada Check Up Plus provides premium assistance to parents or guardians with income below 200 percent of the Federal poverty level or those whose children are eligible for Medicaid or Nevada Check Up. To qualify, the parents must work for a small employer (with two to 50 employees) with an employer contribution of at least 50 percent of health care premiums. The program provides premium assistance up to $100 per month per parent.

New Hampshire

Other State Health Incentives

New Hampshire has enacted HealthFirst, which requires major insurance carriers to offer a standard wellness plan to businesses with up to 50 employees. The target premium is 10 percent of the prior year's median wage, about $262 per month in 2008.

New Jersey

General Health Tax Incentives

New Jersey permits a deduction for medical expenses, qualified Archer Medical Savings Account contributions (following Federal rules), and health insurance costs of the self-employed.

Other State Health Incentives

New Jersey has a small employer health benefits program to ensure that small employers have access to small group health benefits plans. A small employer is defined as one that employs an average of at least two, but not more than 50 eligible employees on business days during the preceding calendar year. Eligible employees are those who work at least 25 hours per week. At least 75 percent of a small employer's eligible employees must participate in coverage. The small employer is required to pay 10 percent of the total cost of the health benefits plan.

New Mexico

General Health Tax Incentives

New Mexico allows a deduction for self-employed health insurance expenses for state individual income tax purposes. New Mexico allows a deduction for individual income tax purposes for medical expenses not included in itemized deductions for Federal return, including unreimbursed and uncompensated medical care expenses. Reimbursed and compensated insurance premiums like those paid with pre-tax dollars under cafeteria and similar benefit plans are not eligible for the deduction.

Other State Health Incentives

New Mexico provides a premium assistance program (State Coverage Insurance) for individuals with income below 200 percent of the Federal poverty level. The program applies to health insurance offered by small businesses with no more than 50 employees and that have not offered health insurance in at least 12 months. The program sets guidelines for the employer and employee contributions based on the employee income. The program has currently reached its maximum enrollment and, as of December 19, 2009, all employer group applicants were being placed on a waiting list.

New York

General Health Tax Incentives

New York allows a deduction for self-employed health insurance expenses and exclusion for employer-provided health insurance for state income tax purposes.

Other State Health Incentives

Healthy NY, a subsidized reinsurance pool, provides lower cost health insurance for low-income individuals and small businesses (with 50 or fewer employees) that meet specific eligibility criteria concerning low-income employees. The small business must not have provided health insurance to employees in the last 12 months. At least 30 percent of the firm's employees must earn $40,000 or less in annual wages (adjusted for inflation). In order to participate in the program, employers must contribute at least 50 percent of the employees' premiums, certify that at least 50 percent of employees offered health insurance will accept it or have health insurance through another source, and must offer health insurance to all employees who work at least 20 hours per week and earn $40,000 per year or less. Healthy NY offers a high deductible health plan that qualifies to be used with a Health Savings Account.

North Carolina

General Health Tax Incentives
North Carolina allows a deduction for self-employed health insurance expenses and exclusion for employer-provided health insurance for state income tax purposes.

Small Business Tax Incentives
Effective for the 2007, 2008, and 2009 tax years, small businesses with no more than 25 employees are eligible to claim a small business health insurance credit against North Carolina corporate or personal income tax or corporation franchise tax if they provide health benefits to all eligible employees. For purposes of the credit, a taxpayer provides health benefits if it pays at least 50 percent of the premiums for health care coverage that equals or exceeds the minimum provisions of the basic health care plan of coverage recommended by the Small Employer Carrier Committee or if its employees have qualifying existing coverage. The credit may only be claimed for health insurance premiums paid for eligible employees whose total annual wages received from the business do not exceed $40,000. The credit is equal to the lesser of $250 or the costs incurred. Taxpayers must make an irrevocable election regarding the tax against which the credit will be claimed when filing the return on which the first credit installment is claimed. Any carry forward of a credit must be claimed against the same tax. All Article 3B credits, including carryovers, may not exceed 50 percent of the tax against which they are claimed for the taxable year. Unused credit may be carried over for five years. The credit expires for taxable years beginning on or after January 1, 2010.

North Dakota

General Health Tax Incentives
North Dakota allows a deduction for self-employed health insurance expenses and exclusion for employer-provided health insurance for state income tax purposes.

Ohio

General Health Tax Incentives

Ohio allows a deduction for self-employed health insurance expenses and exclusion for employer-provided health insurance for state income tax purposes. Ohio also allows a deduction for (1) unsubsidized health care insurance premiums and excess health care expenses, and (2) contributions (up to $4,197 for 2009) to, and earnings of, a Medical Savings Account.

Oklahoma

General Health Tax Incentives

Oklahoma allows a deduction for self-employed health insurance expenses and exclusion for employer-provided health insurance for state income tax purposes. An exemption from income for state tax purposes is provided for contributions to, and interest earned on, an Oklahoma Medical Savings Account and for contributions to, and interest earned on, an Oklahoma Health Savings Account.

Small Business Tax Incentives

Oklahoma offers a refundable tax credit for employers in basic health plans. The credit is $15 per month per employee for up to 2 years. An employer is eligible if the employer (1) has done business in Oklahoma for at least one year, (2) has not provided group health insurance in the previous 15 months, (3) offers a state-certified basic health benefit plan to all eligible employees, and (4) pays 50 percent of the premium for the employee. An eligible employee is one who works an average of 24 hours per week or more for the employer and was not covered by a group health insurance policy within the 15 months preceding the offer to purchase health insurance.

Other State Health Incentives

Oklahoma pays a portion of health plan premiums for eligible employees through its Insure Oklahoma program. This program is offered to businesses with two to 99 employees (but the program may be extended to employers with up to 250 full-time employees). As of September 2008 the program had approximately 10,000 employees enrolled and uses competition among private insurance carriers to keep costs as low as possible. To participate, employees must meet income guidelines (250 percent of the Federal poverty level) and must contribute up to 15 percent of premium costs. The business must offer a qualified health plan and contribute at least 25 percent of employee premiums. The state pays 60 percent of the insurance costs and the employee pays the remaining 15 percent.

Oregon

General Health Tax Incentives
Oregon allows a deduction for self-employed health insurance expenses and exclusion for employer-provided health insurance for state income tax purposes. In addition, Oregon provides a special medical deduction for taxpayers age 62 or older.

Other State Health Incentives
Oregon provides rules regulating the sale of health insurance to employers with two to 50 employees, which require insurance companies to sell to small employers irrespective of their employees' health and using the same rate-setting factors for all small employer groups. Employers who purchase these plans must offer health insurance to all employees who meet minimum service requirements. Insurers may require employers to contribute up to 100 percent of the cost of the health insurance.

Pennsylvania

General Health Tax Incentives
Pennsylvania allows a deduction for self-employed health insurance expenses and exclusion for employer-provided health insurance for state income tax purposes. Pennsylvania also allows deductions for personal income tax purposes for Medical Savings Account contributions and Health Savings Account contributions.

Rhode Island

General Health Tax Incentives
Rhode Island allows a deduction for self-employed health insurance expenses and exclusion for employer-provided health insurance for state income tax purposes.

State's Use of Cafeteria Plans to Provide Health Insurance
In 2007, Rhode Island became the first state to require employers (with 25 or more employees) to offer employees the opportunity to purchase health insurance with pre-tax income (a "stand-alone" cafeteria plan). Neither the state nor employers are required to contribute to the purchase price, but the state estimated premium savings of up to 40 percent depending upon an employee's tax bracket. The plan was implemented in July 2009.

Other State Health Incentives
Rhode Island offers small businesses an affordable product that emphasizes healthier lifestyles. This program offers lower-premium and lower-deductible health insurance through the small group market to businesses of 50 or fewer employees whose workers agree to abide by five preventive health behaviors: complete a health risk assessment; select a primary care physician; pledge to remain at a healthy weight or participate in weight management programs, if morbidly obese; pledge to remain smoke free or participate in smoking cessation programs; and pledge to participate in disease management programs if applicable. Members who opt for these plans participate in regular assessments. If they do not comply with the requirements, their deductibles are increased to non-discounted levels. The programs premiums are about 15 percent to 20 percent lower than comparable plans. Enrollment is limited to 5,000 individuals per insurer with three insurer's offering insurance.

South Carolina

General Health Tax Incentives
South Carolina allows a deduction for self-employed health insurance expenses and exclusion for employer-provided health insurance for state income tax purposes.

Individuals are provided a nonrefundable credit for replacement health insurance coverage. Individuals who held a health insurance policy with an insurer that withdrew from writing policies in South Carolina and, as a result, were assigned to the South Carolina Health Insurance Pool, are entitled to a credit for 50 percent of the premium costs paid during a year for health insurance coverage. The credit cannot exceed $3,000 for each qualifying person covered.

South Dakota

South Dakota does not offer any tax incentives.

Tennessee

General Health Tax Incentives

Tennessee allows a deduction for self-employed health insurance expenses and exclusion for employer-provided health insurance for state income tax purposes.

State's Use of Cafeteria Plans to Provide Health Insurance

Tennessee enacted a law that provides that any employer that has implemented a cafeteria plan must arrange for employee health insurance premiums and dental insurance premiums to be automatically paid through the cafeteria plan beginning January 1, 2008.

Other State Health Incentives

Cover Tennessee (CoverTN) is a partnership between the state, employers, and individuals to offer small businesses guaranteed, affordable basic health coverage. The state, the employer and the employee each pay one-third of premium costs, which vary depending on the age, smoking status and weight of the employee. Monthly premiums vary from $37 to $109. Plans focus on a basic benefit package and encourage regular doctor visits and preventive screenings. The plans do not have an out-of-pocket maximum. The insurance is portable, so members can continue with the same insurance plan even if their place of employment changes. To be eligible, small businesses must have 25 or fewer full-time employees and half of the workforce must make less than 250 percent of the Federal poverty level. Effective December 1, 2009,

CoverTN has been suspended until further notice because the state reached its budget capacity.

Texas

Other State Health Incentives

Texas law allows insurance companies to sell a wide array of small employer health care coverage plans and packages. The term "small employer" means a business with two to 50 eligible employees. The law provides these businesses added protections, including a 15 percent annual cap on rate increases related to health factors, a guarantee that carriers cannot arbitrarily discontinue coverage, and a provision that allows small employers to pool their purchasing clout to negotiate lower insurance rates. For employees of small businesses, the law provides several ways to maintain benefits after leaving a job and limits the waiting period before a health plan will cover pre-existing conditions. Beyond these requirements, small-employer carriers may offer a wide variety of plans, with virtually any combination of features and benefits.

Utah

General Health Tax Incentives

Utah allows a deduction for self-employed health insurance expenses and exclusion for employer-provided health insurance for state income tax purposes. Under Utah law, individuals may claim a credit of 5 percent of the amount paid for a health benefit plan only if the individual, spouse, or dependent is not insured under a health benefit plan maintained by an employer. The credit is not available for amounts that are excluded from income for Federal tax purposes. The maximum credit is $300 per individual.

A credit is allowed for Utah individual income tax for contributions to Medical Savings Accounts that were not deducted on the individual's Federal income tax return.

State's Use of Cafeteria Plans to Provide Health Insurance

An employer that chooses to establish a defined contribution arrangement to provide a health benefit plan for employees is required to provide a pre-tax contribution including a cafeteria plan.

Other State Health Incentives
Utah established the Utah Health Insurance Exchange, which allows small employers with up to 50 employees to buy a choice of health insurance policies.

Vermont

General Health Tax Incentives
Vermont allows a deduction for self-employed health insurance expenses and an exclusion for employer-provided health insurance for state income tax purposes. In addition, Vermont allows a deduction for contributions to Health Savings Accounts for state individual income tax purposes.

Other State Health Incentives
Vermont imposes an employer assessment (fee) for every full-time equivalent employee who is either not offered health insurance or is not enrolled in offered insurance and is uninsured. The first eight qualifying full-time equivalent employees are exempt from the assessment in 2007 and 2008, first six in 2009, and first four in 2010 and thereafter. The assessment is based on FTEs at the rate of $102.20 per quarter ($404.80 per year). The assessment rate will increase annually, based upon premium growth.

Virginia

General Health Tax Incentives
Virginia allows a deduction for self-employed health insurance expenses and exclusion for employer-provided health insurance for state income tax purposes.

Washington

State's Use of Cafeteria Plans to Provide Health Insurance
Under the Health Insurance Partnership (HIP), participating small business employers are required to offer a cafeteria plan. The state-run partnership provides cafeteria plan "technical assistance" to small employers.

Other State Health Incentives

The HIP combines contributions from small employers, employees and the State of Washington to make small group health insurance coverage affordable for employees. The program offers a premium subsidy to eligible employees, based on their family income. Eligible small employers are those with two to 50 employees, the majority of whose employees earn no more than $10 per hour, and which does not currently offer health insurance to its employees. Budget constraints delayed program implementation, but a Federal grant allowed the state to resume work on the program and it is expected to be operational on September 1, 2010.

West Virginia

General Health Tax Incentives

West Virginia allows a deduction for self-employed health insurance expenses and exclusion for employer-provided health insurance for state income tax purposes. In addition, West Virginia allows a deduction for corporate income tax purposes for employer contributions to Medical Savings Accounts included in Federal taxable income. The amount of the deduction may not exceed the maximum amount that would have been deductible from the corporation's Federal taxable income if the aggregate amount of the contributions to individual Medical Savings Accounts were permitted under Federal law.

West Virginia offers an Economic Opportunity Tax Credit for Jobs Creation. An employer in an eligible industry (manufacturing, warehousing, information processing, goods distribution, destination tourism, and research and development) creating less than 20 new jobs for a regular employer and less than 10 new jobs for a qualified small business is eligible for an annual credit of $3,000 per new employee for five years. The new jobs must be full-time, pay a minimum salary of $32,000, and offer health benefits. The credit is first applied to the business and occupation tax, then the business franchise tax, the corporation net income tax, and the personal income tax.

Other State Health Incentives

West Virginia allows small businesses to tap into the purchasing power of the Public Employees Insurance Agency (PEIA) through a public/private partnership with insurance companies. This program saves money by allowing private insurance carriers' access to PEIA physician and provider reimbursement rates, with the insurance carriers assuming risk and taking smaller administrative fees but potentially gaining more small business customers. Eligible employers must have two to 50 employees, been without a company-sponsored health insurance plan for at least 12 months, been in operation for at least one year, and have a minimum of 75 percent of eligible employees sign up for the plan; the employer must pay at least 50 percent of the cost of individual coverage. Premiums costs in West Virginia's program are 17 to 22 percent lower than the usual market rate for small businesses.

Wisconsin

General Health Tax Incentives

Wisconsin allows a deduction for self-employed health insurance expenses and an exclusion for employer-provided health insurance for state income tax purposes. Wisconsin does not allow individuals to claim deductions for contributions to Health Savings Accounts.

Wisconsin allows a deduction for all or a portion of the amount paid by an individual taxpayer for medical care insurance, but the individual cannot include amounts not included in gross income, such as contributions to a cafeteria plan or flexible spending arrangement.

Wyoming

No special tax or special health insurance incentives.

APPENDIX D. SOURCES OF DATA RELATING TO HEALTH INSURANCE ACCESS AND COVERAGE IN THE UNITED STATES

A variety of data sources provide information on health insurance access and coverage in the United States. The data sources often provide different ways to examine the issue relating to health insurance coverage and medical care in general. Thus, each data source offers a different way of looking at the issue of health care access and coverage in the United States. However, it is important to understand both the benefits of, and limitations to, each data source. This appendix provides a brief overview of some of the primary data sources utilized in this paper.

Current Population Survey

The Current Population Survey (CPS) is a monthly survey of approximately 50,000 households in the United States. The Bureau of the Census and the Bureau of Labor Statistics (BLS) jointly conduct the CPS. This survey is the primary source of information on the labor force characteristics of the U.S. population, including employment, unemployment, earnings, and hours of employment. Supplemental questions produce estimates relating to income, previous work experience, school enrollment, employee benefits, and other issues.

The Annual Social and Economic Supplement (ASEC) to the CPS asks questions about health insurance coverage during the prior calendar year.[86] The survey asks questions about the various types of possible health insurance coverage, private or government. For this purpose, private health insurance includes a plan provided through an employer or union (employment-based coverage) or purchased by an individual from a private company (direct purchase). Government health insurance includes coverage under Federal programs, such as Medicare, Medicaid, military health care, the Children's Health Insurance Program (SCHIP), and individual state health plans. If the individual answers no to each of the coverage questions, the survey then asks the individual to verify that the household was not, in fact, covered by health insurance during the prior year. The survey classifies people as "covered" by health insurance if they had any coverage for all or part of the preceding year. Thus, under this survey, people are treated as uninsured only if they do not report any type of health insurance coverage during the entire prior calendar year.

However, research shows that survey respondents tend to underreport health insurance coverage trends in the CPS ASEC. People may forget health insurance coverage that they had at a point in time during the prior year, because of the time difference between having coverage and conducting the survey.[87] Further, some people may report their health insurance coverage at the time of the interview, rather than reporting their coverage during the prior year. Compared with other health insurance surveys, the CPS ASEC estimates of the number of people without health insurance tend to approximate the number of people who were uninsured at a specific time during the year rather than the people who were without health insurance for the entire year.

Medical Expenditure Panel Survey

Beginning in 1996, the Medical Expenditure Panel Survey (MEPS) is a set of large-scale surveys of families and individuals, their medical providers, and employers in the United States conducted by the United States Department of Health and Human Services, Agency for Healthcare Research and Quality.[88] There are two major components to the MEPS – the Household Component and the Insurance Component, as well as smaller components, including the Medical Provider Component and the Nursing Home Component. This research uses data from the Medical Expenditure Panel Survey – Insurance Component (MEPS-IC).

The MEPS-IC is an annual survey of establishments that collects information concerning the offering of employment-based health insurance in the United States.[89] This survey relies on a nationally representative sample of employers developed from Census Bureau data. Survey data are collected at the establishment level, which is defined as a particular workplace or physical location here business is conducted or services or industrial operations are performed. A firm is a business entity consisting of one or more establishments. In the case of a single location firm, the firm and the establishment are identical. The survey data are collected during the year for which the data are relevant and published the following year.

The MEPS-IC survey data compiles estimates (by firm size, by industry, and by establishment characteristics) that provide the following information:

- Establishment-based data such as the percent of establishments that offer health insurance;
- Employee-based data, such as the percent of employees that enroll in health insurance plans;
- Total premiums and employee contributions for premiums, including averages and percentile distributions; and
- Deductibles and copayments for enrollees.

While the MEPS-IC data are collected and presented at the establishment level, establishments are categorized for size purposes based on the size of the firm of which an establishment is a part. This approach allows a small establishment that is part of a large national chain to be categorized as part of a large firm.

In addition to national estimates, the MEPS-IC sample has been large enough since 2003 to permit estimates for all 50 states and the District of Columbia. In 1996, estimates were made for the most populous 40 states. From 1997-2002, estimates were done for the 20 least populated states on a rotating basis. Table D1 shows the smaller states for which estimates are not available for 1996-2002.

In addition, since 2002, the MEPS-IC sample and design supports a limited number of private-sector metropolitan-level estimates.

Table D1. States with Smaller Populations for Which MEPS-IC Estimates are Not Available, 1996–2002

State	1996	1997	1998	1999	2000	2001	2002
Alaska		x				x	
Arkansas	x	x	x	x	x	x	
Delaware			x			x*	x
District of Columbia		x				x	
Hawaii	x	x		x		x	x*
Idaho		x				x	
Kansas	x	x	x	x	x	**	x
Maine	x	x		x		x	x*
Mississippi	x	x		x	x	x	x
Montana				x			x*
Nebraska	x		x	x	x		x
Nevada	x	x		x		x	x
New Hampshire			x		x	**	x
New Mexico	x		x		x		x
North Dakota					x		
Rhode Island		x		x		x	
South Dakota					x	**	
Utah	x	x	x		x	x	x
Vermont				x		x*	
West Virginia	x		x		x		x
Wyoming			x				x

* States received an additional sample that supported a full set of state estimates not otherwise possible.

** States received an additional sample that supported estimates for smaller firms only.

Note: An x indicates that State-level estimates are available for that year; a blank indicates that there are no estimates for that year.

Survey of Income and Program Participation

The Survey of Income and Program Participation (SIPP) is a continuous series of national panel surveys conducted by the U.S. Census Bureau. The SIPP has sample sizes of 14,000 to 36,700 U.S. households. The purpose of the SIPP is to collect information on the source and amount of income, labor force information, program participation and eligibility, and general demographic characteristics.

The SIPP is a longitudinal survey that collects information on topics such as poverty, income, employment and health insurance coverage. Like the CPS, the SIPP is a household survey. Because the SIPP uses different sample sizes, interview techniques, sample compositions, and survey reference periods than the CPS, the two surveys produce varying estimates of health insurance coverage. For example, the SIPP collects information monthly whereas the CPS ASEC is collected once per calendar year several months following the end of the year. Some researchers believe that the CPS estimates are more useful as a point-in-time estimate, whereas the SIPP produces a more accurate annual estimate.[90]

Kaiser Family Foundation Annual Survey of Employer Health Benefits

The Kaiser Family Foundation and the Health Research and Educational Trust (HRET) (a nonprofit research organization that is an affiliate of the American Hospital Association) conduct an annual survey of employer-sponsored health benefits.[91] The 2009 survey was conducted between March and May of 2009 and included 3,199 randomly selected private and public firms with three or more employees (2,054 firms responded to the full survey and an additional 1,134 firms responded to a question concerning the offering of health insurance). The survey contains as many as 400 questions. The sample strata are by industry and number of workers in the firm. In identifying firms for the sample, the survey attempts to repeat interviews with prior years' survey respondents who had at least 10 employees and who had participated in either the 2007 or 2008 survey.

The Kaiser/HRET survey asks questions relating to the:

- costs of health insurance,
- health benefits access rates,

- employee coverage, eligibility, and participation,
- types of plans offered,
- market shares of health plans,
- employee and employer contributions for premiums,
- employee cost sharing,
- high-deductible health plans with savings option,
- prescription drug benefits,
- plan funding,
- retiree health benefits,
- wellness programs and health risk assessments, and
- employer and health plan practices and employer opinions.

The Kaiser/HRET survey identifies small employers as those with 3 to 199 workers and large employers as those with 200 or more workers. In some cases, there is further delineation by employer size in the Kaiser/HRET survey to identify characteristics of employers with 3 to 9 employees, 10 to 24 employees, 25 to 49 employees, 50 to 199 employees, 200 to 999 employees, 1,000 to 4,999 workers, and 5,000 or more employees.

APPENDIX E. MAPS DEPICTING PERCENT OF PRIVATE SECTOR ESTABLISHMENTS THAT OFFER HEALTH INSURANCE, BY FIRM SIZE

While access to employer-sponsored health insurance increases with the size of the firm, there are also regional variations in access to employer-sponsored health insurance as well. Across all small firm size categories, these regional variations tend to show higher access rates in the Northeast and lower access rates in the South. The following maps (E5 to E9) show access rates to employer-sponsored health insurance for various small firm categories.

Some anomalies can be observed. For example, California has one of the highest access rates (42.1 percent and above) for establishments of firms of fewer than 10 employees, but has one of the lowest access rates (90 percent and below) for establishments of firms with 100 to 499 employees. Montana, on the other hand, has one of the lowest access rates for establishments of firms of fewer than 10 employees, but has a fairly high access rate (96.1 to 97.7 percent) for establishments of firms with 100 to 499 employees.

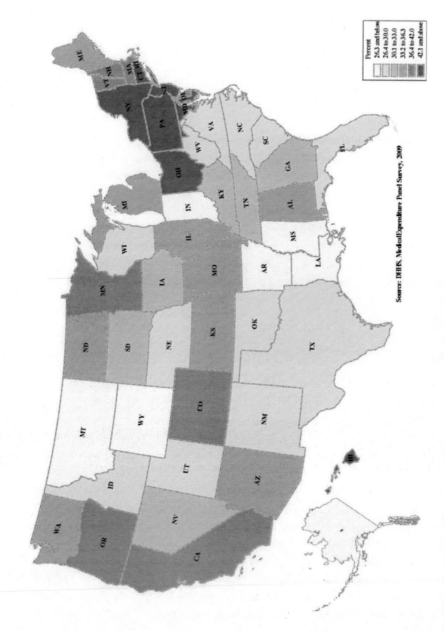

Source: DHHS, Medical Expenditure Panel Survey, 2009

Percent
26.3 and below
26.4 to 30.0
30.1 to 33.0
33.2 to 36.3
36.4 to 42.0
42.1 and above

Map E1. Percent of Private-Sector Establishments that Offer Health Insurance, Firm Size of Fewer than 10 Employees, 2009.

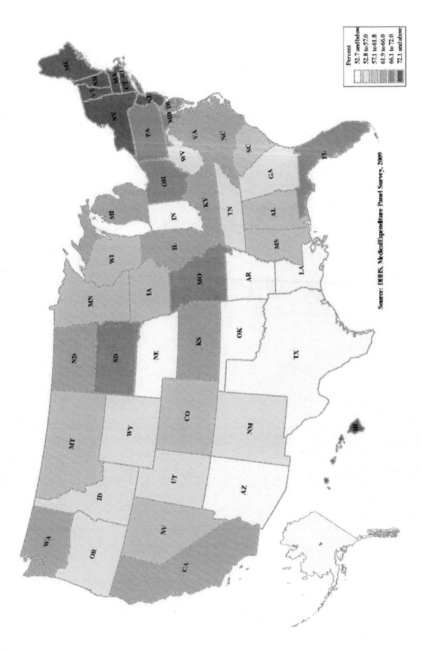

Map E2. Percent of Private-Sector Establishments that Offer Health Insurance, Firm Size of Fewer than 10 Employees, 2009.

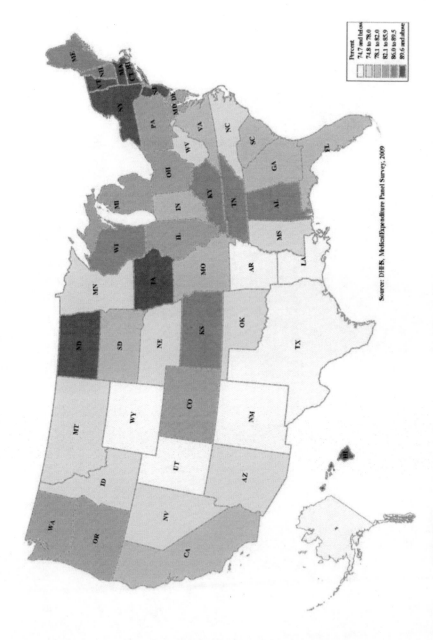

Percent

- 74.7 and below
- 74.8 to 78.0
- 78.1 to 82.0
- 82.1 to 85.9
- 86.0 to 89.5
- 89.6 and above

Map E3. Percent of Private-Sector Establishments that Offer Health Insurance, Firm Size of 25 to 99 Employees, 2009.

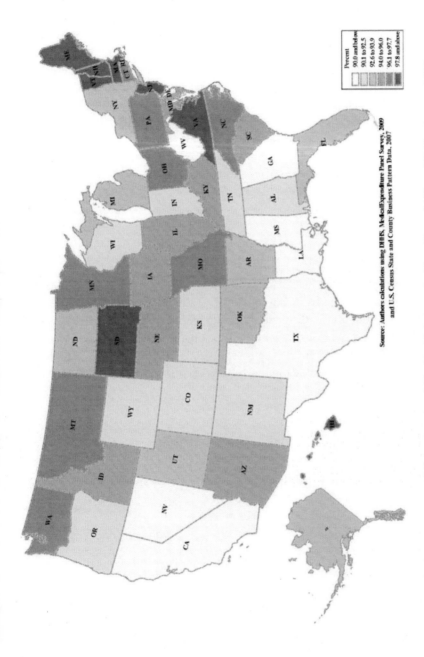

Percent
☐ 90.0 and below
☐ 90.1 to 92.5
☐ 92.6 to 93.9
☐ 94.0 to 96.0
☐ 96.1 to 97.7
☐ 97.8 and above

Source: Authors calculations using DHHS, Medical Expenditure Panel Survey, 2009
and U.S. Census State and County Business Pattern Data, 2007

Map E4. Percent of Private-Sector Establishments that Offer Health Insurance, Firm Size of 100 to 499 Employees, 2009.

There are likely a number of reasons that these regional variations in access occur. An Urban Institute analysis demonstrated that coverage by private health insurance (which is predominantly employer-sponsored health insurance) declines as the county of an individual's residence becomes more remote.[92] This analysis identified Mississippi as the most rural state, with 53.7 percent of Mississippi residents living in counties that were not adjacent to an urban area. Consistent with the Urban Institute analysis, Maps E-5 to E9 show that Mississippi has among the lowest access rates in the country. The Urban Institute analysis notes that employer-sponsored health insurance is less common in rural areas because of great prevalence of small businesses, lower wages, and high rates of self-employment.

BIBLIOGRPAHY

[1] Auerbach, David, Janet Holtzblatt, Paul Jacobs, Alexandra Minicozzi, Pamela Moomau & Chapin White. (2010). *Will Health Insurance Mandates Increase Coverage?*, Congressional Budget Office Working Paper Series, Working Paper 2010-05, August.

[2] Baer, David & Ellen O'Brien. (2009). *Federal and State Income Tax Incentives for Private Long-Term Care Insurance*, AARP Public Policy Institute, November.

[3] Bhandari, Shailesh. (2004). *"People with Health Insurance: A Comparison of Estimates from Two Surveys,"* Survey of Income and Program Participation Report No. 243, June 8, at http://www.sipp. census.gov/sipp/workpapr/wp243.pdf.

[4] Blakeley, Stephen. (2010). *Employers, Workers, and the Future of Employment-Based Health Insurance.* Employee Benefit Research Institute, Issue Brief No. 339, February.

[5] Blumberg, Linda J. (1999). *Who Pays for Employer Sponsored Health Insurance? Evidence and Policy Implications.* Health Affairs, Vol. 18, No. 6, November/December.

[6] Blumberg, Linda J. & Stacey McMorrow. (2009). *What Would Health Care Reform Mean for Small Employers and Their Workers?* Timely Analysis of Immediate Health Policy Issues, Robert Wood Johnson Foundation and the Urban Institute, December.

[7] Blumenthal, David. (2006). *Employer-Sponsored Health Insurance in the United States – Origins and Implications.* New England Journal of Medicine, *355*, 1, July 6.

[8] Chu, Rose C. & Trapnell, Gordon R. (2003). *Study of the Administrative Costs and Actuarial Values of Small Health Plans.* U.S. Small Business Administration, Office of Advocacy, January.

[9] Clemans-Cope, Lisa, Genevieve Kenney & Aaron Lucas. (2010). *Health Insurance in Nonstandard Jobs and Small Firms: Differences for Parents by Race and Ethnicity.* The Urban Institute, Brief 12, April.

[10] DeNavas-Walt, Carmen, Proctor, Bernadette D. & Smith, Jessica C. (2009). U.S. Census Bureau, Current Population Reports, P60-236, *Income, Poverty, and Health Insurance Coverage in the United States: 2008.* U.S. Government Printing Office, Washington, DC, September.

[11] Employee Benefits Research Service, Issue Brief (2009). *Sources of Health Insurance and Characteristics of the Uninsured: Analysis of the March 2009 Current Population Survey,* No. 334, September.

[12] Employee Benefits Research Service, Notes (2009). *Health Insurance Coverage of Individuals Ages 55–64, 1994–2007,* Vol. *30*, No. 8, August.

[13] Employee Benefits Research Service, Fast Facts (2009). *Health Plan Differences: Fully-Insured vs. Self-Insured,* No. 114, February 11.

[14] Families USA and the Small Business Majority (2010). *A Helping Hand for Small Businesses. Health Insurance Tax Credits.* July.

[15] Feder, Lester & Ellen-Marie Whelan. (2008). *Small Businesses, Large Problems: Health Care Costs Hit Small Employers,* Center for American Progress, October 30, available at http://www.americanprogress.org/issues/2008/10/small_business_brief.html.

[16] Fronstin, Paul. (2010). *The Impact of the Recession on Employment-Based Health Coverage.* Employee Benefit Research Institute, Issue Brief No. 342, May.

[17] Fronstin, Paul. (2009). *Capping the Tax Exclusion for Employment-Based Health Coverage: Implications for Employers and Workers.* Employee Benefits Research Institute Issue Brief No. 325, January.

[18] Fronstin, Paul (2007). *Employment-Based Health Benefits: Access and Coverage, 1988-2005,* Employee Benefits Research Institute, Issue Brief No. 303, March.

[19] Headd, Brian. (2000). *The Characteristics of Small-Business Employees.* Monthly Labor Review, April.

[20] Hirth, Richard A., Reagan Baughman, Michael Chernew & Emily Shelton. (2006). *Worker Preferences, Sorting and Aggregate Patterns of Health Insurance Coverage.* February 9.

[21] Holahan, John & Bowen, Garrett, A. (2009). *Rising Unemployment, Medicaid and the Uninsured,* Kaiser Commission on Medicaid and the Uninsured, January. Accessed at www.kff.org/uninsured/upload/7850. pdf .

[22] Insure Montana Small Business Insurance Program Newsletter (2009). Volume *4*, Issue 2, September 1, available at www.sao.mt.gov/ InsureMontana/PDF/NewslettersSept09.pdf .

[23] Kaiser Family Foundation (2010). *Comparison of Expenditures in Nongroup and Employer-Sponsored Insurance: 2004-2007,* March. Accessed at www.kff.org/insurance/snapshot/chcm111006oth.cfm .

[24] Kaiser Family Foundation, statehealthfacts.org.

[25] Kaiser Family Foundation (2009). *Snapshots: Health Care Costs. Wages and Benefits: A Long-Term View.* November. Accessed at: www.kff.org/ insurance/snapshot/chcm012808oth.cfm .

[26] Kaiser Family Foundation and Health Research and Educational Trust, *Employer Health Benefits Survey, 2009 Annual Survey,* available at http://ehbs.kff.org/pdf/2009/7936.pdf .

[27] Lueck, Sarah. (2010). *States Should Structure Insurance Exchanges to Minimize Adverse Selection.* Center on Budget and Policy Priorities, August 17, available at http://www.cbpp.org/files/8-17-10health.pdf.

[28] Lyke, Bob. (2008). *The Tax Exclusion for Employer-Provided Health Insurance. Policy Issues Regarding the Repeal Debate.* CRS Report for Congress. Congressional Research Service, November 21.

[29] Ormond, Barbara A., Stephen Zuckerman & Apama Lhila. (2000). *Rural/Urban Differences in Health Care Are Not Uniform Across States,* Urban Institute, Series B, No. B-11, May.

[30] Peterson, Chris L. & Hinda Chaikind. (2010). *Summary of Small Business Health Insurance Tax Credit Under PPACA (P.L. 111-148).* Congressional Research Service, CRS Report for Congress, R41158, April 20.

[31] Sommers, John P. & Beth Levin Crimmel. *Co-Pays, Deductibles, and Coinsurance Percentages for Employer-Sponsored Health Insurance in the Private Sector, by Firm Size Classification, 2006.* U.S. Department of Health and Human Services, Agency for Healthcare Research and Quality, Statistical Brief #216.

[32] U.S. Bureau of the Census, Income, Poverty, and Health Insurance Coverage in the United *States: 2009,* March 2010 Supplement to the Current Population Survey, issued September 2010.

[33] U.S. Bureau of the Census, Current Population Survey, March 2009 Supplement to the Current Population Survey.

[34] U.S. Bureau of the Census, Current Population Survey, March 2008 Supplement to the Current Population Survey.

[35] U.S. Congress, Joint Committee on Taxation, *Tax Expenditures for Health Care*, JCX-66-08, July 31, 2008.

[36] U.S. Congressional Budget Office, The Effects Of Health Reform on the Federal Budget, presented by Douglass W. Elmendorf, Director to the World Health Care Congress, April 12, 2010.

[37] U.S. Department of Labor, Bureau of Labor Statistics, National Compensation Survey, March 2010.

[38] U.S. Department of Labor, Bureau of Labor Statistics, *Employers Costs for Employee Compensation – March 2010*, USDL-10-0774, June 9, 2010.

[39] U.S. Department of Health and Human Services, Agency for Healthcare Research and Quality, Medical Expenditure Panel Survey, 2009.

[40] U.S. Department of Health and Human Services, Agency for Healthcare Research and Quality, *MEPS Insurance Component: Technical Notes and Survey Documentation.* http://www.meps.ahrq.gov/mepsweb/survey _comp/ic_technical_notes.shtml.

[41] U.S. Department of Health and Human Services, Agency for Healthcare Research and Quality, Statistical Brief #209, July 2008.

[42] U.S. Small Business Administration. *Table of Small Business Size Standards Matched to North American Industry Classification System Codes.* Effective November 5, 2010.

[43] U.S. Treasury Department, Internal Revenue Service, Statistics of Income, Individual Income Tax Return Data, Tax Years 1998 through 2008.

[44] U.S. Treasury Department, Internal Revenue Service, Statistics of Income, Corporate Source Book Data, 2003 through 2007 editions.

End Notes

[1] See the discussion below concerning economic theory concerning whether the employer or employee bears the burden of the employer share of payroll taxes.

[2] The Small Business Administration generally defines small businesses, for SBA financial assistance and other programs and for Federal government procurement programs, as those firms with no more than 500 employees or receipts no greater than $7 million, although the size standards vary by industry and can be larger or smaller than the general standards

depending upon the industry. See U.S. Small Business Administration, Table of Size Standards Matched to North American Industry Classification System Codes. The IRS uses a general classification of assets less than $10 million to distinguish small businesses. This study generally uses a size standard of less than 500 employees as a definition of a small business because most of the reliable survey data are collected based on establishment or firm size, except that the study uses the IRS definition of assets of less than $10 million to identify small corporations. In certain circumstances, when imputation was not possible, the analysis in this paper may present data that relies on slightly different business size classifications.

[3] Section 162(l) of the Internal Revenue Code of 1986.

[4] The Census Bureau publishes this data using administrative records from the Internal Revenue Service. Most of the nonemployee firms are sole proprietorships, but there are also some partnerships and corporations that report no employees included in this number. In order to identify legitimate operating businesses, the BLS only includes businesses than have at least $1,000 of annual receipts.

[5] It is difficult to determine the employment status of the tax returns reporting incomes between $10,000 and $20,000; some taxpayers may, in fact, have full-time employment with an employer and earn self-employment income on a part-time basis. In other cases, however, self-employment may be the primary source of income and those taxpayers may have low net incomes (either low income and/or high self-employed deductions).

[6] Tax-exempt employers (i.e., organizations described in section 501(c) of the Internal Revenue Code) can use the credit to offset the amounts withheld for income tax for employees and the employer and employee share of Medicare taxes.

[7] In some cases, surveys show costs of health insurance at the small business level that are comparable to the costs of large businesses, but this often reflects the fact that the health insurance offered to employees at the small business level is less generous than health insurance offered by large businesses.

[8] Medical Expenditure Panel Survey, 2009.

[9] For an excellent overview of the origins of health insurance (and particularly employer-sponsored health insurance) in the United States, see Blumenthal, David. *Employer-Sponsored Health Insurance in the United States – Origins and Implications.* New England Journal of Medicine, 355;1, July 6, 2006. Also see Fronstin, Paul. *Capping the Tax Exclusion for Employment-Based Health Coverage: Implications for Employers and Workers.* Employee Benefits Research Institute Issue Brief No. 325, January 2009.

[10] Fronstin, supra.

[11] Income, Poverty, and Health Insurance Coverage in the United States: 2009, March 2010 Supplement to the Current Population Survey, issued September 2010, and Blakeley, Stephen. *Employers, Workers, and the Future of Employment-Based Health Insurance.* Employee Benefit Research Institute, Issue Brief No. 339, February 2010. See Appendix D for an overview of the data sources available relating to health insurance coverage in the United States.

[12] The CPS survey considers a household to have access to health insurance if they have access to such insurance at any point during the calendar year. Thus, a household could have access to health insurance through more than one source during any calendar year.

[13] Current Population Survey, March 2008 and 2009 Supplements.

[14] Graph 1 displays the sources of health insurance coverage in the United States for 2009. It is important to note that some individuals may have coverage from more than one source. For instance, some individuals that receive their primary health insurance coverage from Medicare may also receive secondary coverage from an employer plan.

[15] *Snapshots: Health Care Costs. Wages and Benefits: A Long-Term View.* The Kaiser Family Foundation, November 2009. Accessed at: www.kff.org/insurance/snapshot/chcm012808 oth.cfm.

[16] Total compensation includes workers compensation and unemployment insurance. These mandated benefits play an important role in the increase in health costs as these costs have increased steadily over time.

[17] *Id.*

[18] The decline in the percentage of compensation costs related to non-health benefits corresponds with the rise in the use of 401(k) plans by employers in lieu of traditional defined benefit pension plans.

[19] *Id.*

[20] Lyke, Bob. *CRS Report for Congress. The Tax Exclusion for Employer-Provided Health Insurance: Policy Issues Regarding the Repeal Debate.* Congressional Research Service, November 21, 2008.

[21] If an employer provides health insurance instead of cash wages to employees, the value of the health insurance benefits provided is not subject to employment taxes (e.g., taxes to help fund Social Security and Medicare). However, as discussed below, economists generally believe that these taxes are ultimately borne by employees, rather than employers; thus, this difference in treatment between health insurance and cash wages should not affect the employer's decision whether to offer health insurance.

[22] The value of health insurance provided to employees is excludable from wages for Federal payroll tax purposes; thus, employers are not required to pay the 6.2 percent of payroll employer share of OASDI taxes on the value of employer-provided health insurance. However, economists generally believe that employees bear the burden of payroll taxes through reduced cash compensation; thus, this tax benefit at least theoretically accrues to employees rather than employers. The only exception to this rule would be employees subject to the Federal minimum wage, as their cash compensation cannot be reduced below the Federal minimum.

[23] Blumberg, Linda J. *Who Pays for Employer Sponsored Health Insurance? Evidence and Policy Implications.* Health Affairs, Vol. 18, No. 6, November/December 1999.

[24] It should be noted that there are other types of employer-provided benefits, such as retirement savings, transit benefits, etc., that provide a similar Federal tax advantage for employees. Thus, there is an interaction between demand for health insurance, demand for cash wages, and demand for other types of benefits. However, for simplicity, the analysis ignores the demand for other types of benefits.

[25] However, in the case of low-wage workers who are subject to the minimum wage, the employee cannot directly bear the burden of these taxes through reduced wages.

[26] A new study in the State of Oregon will actually test the healthiness of individuals with and without health insurance. Results of this study are expected beginning in 2011. For information on this landmark study of people's health and access to care, see www.oregonhealthstudy.org.

[27] *Comparison of Expenditures in Nongroup and Employer-Sponsored Insurance: 2004-2007,* Kaiser Family Foundation, March 2010. Accessed at www.kff.org/insurance/snapshot/chcm111006oth.cfm .

[28] *Id.*

[29] Agency for Healthcare Research and Quality, Center for Financing, Access and Cost Trends, 2009 Medical Expenditure Panel Survey – Insurance Component. In contrast to the data in part A, above, the MEPS data examines health insurance access by private sector establishment, rather than by total private sector workers. An establishment is a particular workplace or physical business location where the business performs services or industrial operations. However, for purposes of classifying establishments by size, firm level data are used. Thus, if a business has more than one establishment, the number of employees in all establishments are aggregated to determine the size of the firm. In the case of many small businesses, the firm and the establishment will be the same. But some employers may have many small establishments that aggregate into a single large firm. Thus, using the firm level

data for size classification purposes provides a better measure of the size of the employer. See Appendix D for a discussion of the various data sources relating to health insurance access and coverage.

[30] See the discussion below concerning the self-employed health insurance deduction, which is relevant for the owners of unincorporated businesses.

[31] Data available from the Bureau of Labor Statistics, National Compensation Survey (NCS) does not offer detailed breakout of establishments with fewer than 50 employees. In addition, the NCS data does not offer a detailed size breakout of employer classes with 500 or more employees. It should be noted that business size is categorized based on the establishment for NCS survey data, whereas business size is categorized based on the firm size for the MEPS-IC survey data.

[32] Fronstin, Paul, "Employment-Based Health Benefits: Access and Coverage, 1988-2005," Employee benefits Research Institute, Issue Brief No. 303, March 2007.

[33] Ibid.

[34] Section 162(l) of the Internal Revenue Code of 1986.

[35] The Census Bureau publishes this data using administrative records from the Internal Revenue Service. Most of the nonemployee firms are sole proprietorships, but there are also some partnerships and corporations that report no employees included in this number. In order to identify legitimate operating businesses, the BLS only includes businesses than have at least $1,000 of annual receipts.

[36] When a taxpayer reports a net loss, the SOI tables classify them as having no net income. To the casual observer, this might suggest a low-income person. In fact, it typically reflects an otherwise high-income taxpayer that experiences unusual losses.

[37] Chu, Rose C. and Trapnell, Gordon R. *Study of the Administrative Costs and Actuarial Values of Small Health Plans.* U.S. Small Business Administration, Office of Advocacy, January 2003.

[38] Sommers, John P. and Crimmel, Beth Levin. *Co-Pays, Deductibles, and Coinsurance Percentages for Employer-Sponsored Health Insurance in the Private Sector, by Firm Size Classification, 2006.* U.S. Department of Health and Human Services, Agency for Healthcare Research and Quality, Statistical Brief #209, July 2008.

[39] Insurance Component of the Medical Expenditure Panel, 2009.

[40] Blumberg, Linda J. and Stacey McMorrow. *What Would Health Care Reform Mean for Small Employers and Their Workers?* Timely Analysis of Immediate Health Policy Issues, Robert Wood Johnson Foundation and the Urban Institute, December 2009.

[41] *Employers Costs for Employee Compensation – March 2010.* Bureau of Labor Statistics, U.S. Department of Labor, USDL-10-0774, June 9, 2010.

[42] *Id.*

[43] *Id.*

[44] Graph 6 displays the mean hourly earnings excluding benefits. Data displayed in Table 5 provide comparable statistics for total compensation, which includes benefits.

[45] A low-income employee's preference for health insurance coverage will also be affected by a number of other factors, such as family status and whether the employee has a spouse has access to health insurance through his or her employer.

[46] Headd, Brian. *The Characteristics of Small-Business Employees.* Monthly Labor Review, April 2000.

[47] A 2006 study by Hirth, et al. explored the issue of whether employees sort themselves into firms with or without health insurance based upon their preferences for cash wages or health insurance coverage. This study noted that workers in firms that do not offer health insurance coverage are more likely to have characteristics associated with low demand for health insurance, which the authors identified as young, male, and having other sources of income. In addition, the research noted that nearly half of small employers cited a lack of demand

for health insurance on the part of their employees as a reason for not offering the coverage. The study concluded that at least some workers sort themselves into firms that meet their preferences for cash wages versus health insurance, but found overall that one out of six uninsured workers in the United States were "involuntarily" uninsured because they worked for firms that did not offer health insurance. Hirth, Richard A., Baughman, Reagan, Chernew, Michael, and Shelton, Emily. *Worker Preferences, Sorting and Aggregate Patterns of Health Insurance Coverage.* February 9, 2006.

[48] Clemans-Cope, Lisa, Kenney, Genevieve, and Lucas, Aaron. *Health Insurance in Nonstandard Jobs and Small Firms: Differences for Parents by Race and Ethnicity.* The Urban Institute, Brief 12, April 2010.

[49] *Id.*

[50] Lueck, Sarah. *States Should Structure Insurance Exchanges to Minimize Adverse Selection.* Center on Budget and Policy Priorities, August 17, 2010. Accessed at http://www.cbpp.org/files/8-17-10health.pdf.

[51] Chu and Trapnell, supra.

[52] Feder, Lester and Whelan, Ellen-Marie. *Small Businesses, Large Problems. Health Care Costs Hit Small Employers.* Center for American Progress, October 30, 2008. Accessed at http://www.americanprogress.org/issues/2008/10/small_business_brief.html.

[53] Holahan, John and Garrett, A. Bowen. *Rising Unemployment, Medicaid and the Uninsured,* Kaiser Commission on Medicaid and the Uninsured, January 2009. Accessed at www.kff.org/uninsured/upload/7850.pdf. Using data from 1990-2003 from the CPS, the authors estimated regression models of coverage rates for employer-sponsored insurance, Medicaid and SCHIP, private health insurance, and no insurance and structured the models to estimate the relationship between each type of coverage and the unemployment rate, holding constant the effects of other factors, such as state health insurance costs and demographic characteristics, that might also have an impact.

[54] *Id.*

[55] Fronstin, Paul. *The Impact of the Recession on Employment-Based Health Coverage.* Employee Benefit Research Institute, EBRI Issue Brief No. 342, May 2010. See also the discussion about the SIPP as a data source on health insurance in Appendix D.

[56] When workers lose employment-based health insurance coverage because they have lost their job, they are entitled to purchase the same coverage for up to 18 months through a continuation of coverage program known as COBRA (named for the Act that enacted the benefit). Employers with 20 or more employees are required to make COBRA coverage available to employees who terminate employment (unless the termination was for gross misconduct). The employee must pay the full amount of the COBRA premium, which equals 100 percent of the cost for similarly situated individuals (including both the employer and employee shares of the cost) plus 2 percent for administrative costs. However, under a provision of the American Recovery and Reinvestment Act of 2009, certain individuals are eligible for a Federal subsidy of 65 percent of the COBRA premium for up to 9 months.

[57] See Appendix C.

[58] Refer to Appendix E for maps showing the employer access rates by state and by employer size.

[59] As of 2009, the National Council of State Legislatures identified these on their website: www.ncls.org/Default.aspx?tabID=13956.

[60] The Kaiser Family Foundation, statehealthfacts.org. Data sources: Agency for Healthcare Research and Quality, Center for Financing, Access and Cost Trends. 2009 MEPS-IC. Tables II.D.1, II.D.2, II.D.3 available at: MEPS , accessed July 15, 2010.

[61] Table 7, above, and 2009 Medical Expenditure Panel Survey, Table II.A.2.

[62] Insure Montana Small Business Insurance Program Newsletter, Volume 4, Issue 2, September 1, 2009, available at www.sao.mt.gov/InsureMontana/PDF/NewslettersSept09.pdf.

[63] In some cases, the states may provide special tax incentives to the employer to offer compensation in the form of benefits rather than wages. See the discussion in Part IV.B.

[64] Refer to the IRS, Statistics of Income, Corporation Source Book, Tax Year 2007, "Returns of Active Corporations." It is not possible to get similar statistics for sole proprietorships and partnerships.

[65] This estimate excludes retirement benefits and other benefits reported with wage and salary expenses. Components of employee benefits for small businesses were from the Bureau of Labor Statistics, Employer Costs for Compensation, prepared from the National Compensation Survey, March 2010 Table 13.

[66] Data for small C and S corporations are used because the IRS does not publish comparable data by asset size for sole proprietorships and partnerships.

[67] The small business definition is those businesses with less than $10 million in assets. Refer to the IRS, Statistics of Income, 2007.

[68] See the Joint Committee on Taxation, Tax Expenditures for Health Care, JCX-66-08, July 31, 2008.

[69] Nonprofit employers may take a smaller credit, allowed against income tax withholding from employee wages and against the employer and employee share of Medicare taxes.

[70] *A Helping Hand for Small Businesses. Health Insurance Tax Credits.* A Report for Families USA and Small Business Majority, July 2010.

[71] See http://www.treasury.gov/press-center/press-releases/Documents/additional%20 background%20on%20the%20small%20business%20health%20care%20tax%20credit.pdf .

[72] Author's calculations based on the 2007 Corporation Source Book of Statistics of Income. Refer to Table 3 – (file 07co03ccr.xls) Balance Sheet, Income Statement and Selected Other Items, by Size of Total Assets, Tax Year 2007 and (file 07sb1ai.xls) Returns of Active Corporation. Data for small C and S corporations are used because the IRS does not publish comparable data by asset size for sole proprietorships and partnerships.

[73] *Testimony of Douglas W. Elmendorf, Director, CBO's Analysis of the Major Health Care Legislation Enacted in March 2010*, Testimony before the Subcommittee on Health, Committee on Energy and Commerce, U.S. House of Representatives, March 30, 2011.

[73] *Testimony of Douglas W. Elmendorf, Director, CBO's Analysis of the Major Health Care Legislation Enacted in March 2010*, Testimony before the Subcommittee on Health, Committee on Energy and Commerce, U.S. House of Representatives, March 30, 2011.

[74] Fronstin, Paul, EBRI Issue Brief No. 342, May 2010 (using SIPP data).

[75] *A Helping Hand for Small Business*, supra.

[76] References to IRC are references to the sections of the applicable law in the Internal Revenue Code of 1986.

[77] In the absence of the cafeteria plan rules, employees who had a choice between a taxable and nontaxable benefit would not be able to exclude the value of the nontaxable benefit from their income.

[78] Employers often pay for only a portion of the cost of employer-provided health insurance coverage and require the employee to contribute the rest of the cost.

[79] In addition, effective for tax years beginning after December 31, 2012, the PPACA changed the definition of permitted medical expenses for FSAs, HRAs, HSAs, and MSAs to exclude doctor prescribed over-the-counter medicines from eligibility for reimbursement on a tax-favored basis.

[80] Individuals enrolled in Medicare Part A or Part B are not permitted to make contributions to an HSA.

[81] An employer must make comparable contributions to HSAs on behalf of all employees with comparable health plan coverage during the same period.

[82] The dollar amounts are for 2010 and are indexed each year for inflation.

[83] Peterson, Chris L. and Chaikind, Hinda. *Summary of Small Business Health Insurance Tax Credit Under PPACA (P.L. 111-148).* Congressional Research Service, CRS Report for Congress, R41158, April 20, 2010.

[84] States that do not have an individual income tax do not have a reason to enact special tax incentives for health insurance. The following states do not have an individual income tax (or have a limited income tax, such as an income tax on interest and dividends only): Alaska, Florida, Nevada, New Hampshire, South Dakota, Tennessee, Texas, Washington, and Wyoming.

[85] Although the Employee Retirement Income Security Act of 1974 (ERISA) generally preempts any state laws relating to the regulation of employer health insurance plans, Hawaii received a statutory exception from ERISA for its state mandate.

[86] DeNavas- Walt, Carmen, Bernadette D. Proctor, and Jessica C. Smith. U.S. Census Bureau, Current Population Reports, P60-236, *Income, Poverty, and Health Insurance Coverage in the United States: 2008*. U.S. Government Printing Office, Washington, DC, September 2009.

[87] The CPS collects responses in February and April of the following year. Therefore, a year or more may pass from the time of coverage and the survey.

[88] MEPS Insurance Component: Technical Notes and Survey Documentation. Agency for Healthcare Research and Quality, Rockville, Md. http://www.meps.ahrq.gov/survey_comp/ic_technical_notes.shtml.

[89] *MEPS Insurance Component: Technical Notes and Survey Documentation.* U.S. Department of Health and Human Services, Agency for Healthcare Research and Quality, Medical Expenditure Panel Survey. http://www.meps.ahrq.gov/mepsweb/survey_comp/ic_technical_notes.shtml.

[90] Bhandari Shailesh, "People with Health Insurance: A Comparison of Estimates from Two Surveys," Survey of Income and Program Participation Report No. 243, June 8, 2004, at http://www.sipp.census.gov/sipp/workpapr/wp243.pdf.

[91] Refer to the Employer Health Benefits Survey, 2009 Annual Survey, Kaiser Family Foundation and Health Research and Educational Trust, 2009, at http://ehbs.kff.org/pdf/2009/7936.pdf.

[92] Ormond, Barbara A., Stephen Zuckerman, and Apama Lhila. *Rural/Urban Differences in Health Care Are Not Uniform Across States.* The Urban Institute, Series B, No. B-11, May 2000.

In: Small Business Health Insurance   ISBN: 978-1-62417-239-7
Editor: Ibrahim N. McCormick   © 2013 Nova Science Publishers, Inc.

Chapter 2

SMALL EMPLOYER HEALTH TAX CREDIT: FACTORS CONTRIBUTING TO LOW USE AND COMPLEXITY*

United States Government Accountability Office

WHY GAO DID THIS STUDY

Many small employers do not offer health insurance. The Small Employer Health Insurance Tax Credit was established to help eligible small employers—businesses or tax-exempt entities—provide health insurance for employees. The base of the credit is premiums paid or the average premium for an employer's state if premiums paid were higher. In 2010, for small businesses, the credit was 35 percent of the base unless the business had more than 10 FTE employees or paid average annual wages over $25,000.

GAO was asked to examine (1) the extent to which the credit is claimed and any factors that limit claims, including how they can be addressed; (2) how fully IRS is ensuring that the credit is correctly claimed; and (3) what data are needed to evaluate the effects of the credit.

GAO compared IRS data on credit claims with estimates of eligible employers, interviewed various credit stakeholders and IRS officials as well as academicians on evaluation, compared IRS credit compliance documents with

---

* This is an edited, reformatted and augmented version of the Highlights of GAO-12-549, a report to congressional requesters, dated May 2012.

the rules and practices used for prior tax provisions and IRS strategic objectives, and reviewed literature and data.

WHAT GAO RECOMMENDS

GAO recommends that IRS (1) improve instructions to examiners working on cases on the credit and (2) analyze results from examinations of credit claimants and use those results to identify and address any errors through alternative approaches. IRS agreed with GAO's recommendations.

WHAT GAO FOUND

Fewer small employers claimed the Small Employer Health Insurance Tax Credit in tax year 2010 than were estimated to be eligible. While 170,300 small employers claimed it, estimates of the eligible pool by government agencies and small business advocacy groups ranged from 1.4 million to 4 million. The cost of credits claimed was $468 million. Most claims were limited to partial rather than full percentage credits (35 percent for small businesses) because of the average wage or full-time equivalent (FTE) requirements. As shown in the figure, 28,100 employers claimed the full credit percentage. In addition, 30 percent of claims had the base premium limited by the state premium average.

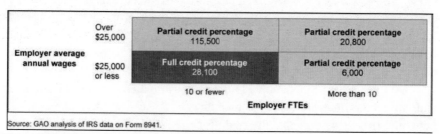

Source: GAO analysis of IRS data on Form 8941.

Notes: This information is based on the approximately 170,300 small employer claims. Numbers are rounded to the nearest hundred. Numbers don't add up because of rounding.

Number of Small Employers Claiming the Full and Partial Credit Percentages, by FTE and Wage Requirements for the Credit, Tax Year 2010.

One factor limiting the credit's use is that most very small employers, 83 percent by one estimate, do not offer health insurance. According to employer representatives, tax preparers, and insurance brokers that GAO met with, the credit was not large enough to incentivize employers to begin offering insurance. Complex rules on FTEs and average wages also limited use. In addition, tax preparer groups GAO met with generally said the time needed to calculate the credit deterred claims. Options to address these factors, such as expanded eligibility requirements, have trade-offs, including less precise targeting of employers and higher costs to the Federal government.

The Internal Revenue Service (IRS) incorporated practices used successfully for prior tax provisions and from IRS strategic objectives into its compliance efforts for the credit. However, the instructions provided to its examiners (1) do not address the credit's eligibility requirements for employers with non-U.S. addresses and (2) have less detail for reviewing the eligibility of tax-exempt entities' health insurance plans compared to those for reviewing small business plans. These omissions may cause examiners to overlook or inconsistently treat possible noncompliance. Further, IRS does not systematically analyze examination results to understand the types of errors and whether examinations are the best way to correct each type. As a result, IRS is less able to ensure that resources target errors with the credit rather than compliant claimants.

Currently available data on health insurance that could be used to evaluate the effects of the credit do not match the credit's eligibility requirements, such as information to convert data on number of employees to FTEs. Additional data that would need to be collected depend on the questions policymakers would want answered and the costs of collecting such data.

ABBREVIATIONS

CBO	Congressional Budget Office
COBRA	Consolidated Omnibus Budget Reconciliation Act
FTE	full-time equivalent
HHS	Department of Health and Human Services
IRS	Internal Revenue Service
JCT	Joint Committee on Taxation
MEA	Math Error Authority
MEPS	Medical Expenditure Panel Survey

NFIB	National Federation of Independent Businesses
PPACA	Patient Protection and Affordable Care Act
SBA	Small Business Administration
SBM	Small Business Majority
SB/SE	Small Business and Self-Employed Division
TEGE	Tax Exempt and Government Entities Division
TETR	Telephone Excise Tax Refund
TIGTA	Treasury Inspector General for Tax Administration

May 14, 2012

The Honorable Olympia J. Snowe
Ranking Member
Committee on Small Business and Entrepreneurship
United States Senate

The Honorable Sam Graves
Chairman
Committee on Small Business
House of Representatives

Many small employers do not offer health insurance to their employees. This is particularly true for small employers paying low wages. According to data from the Medical Expenditure Panel Survey (MEPS)[1] about 17 percent of employers with less than 10 employees who earn low wages (50 percent or more of their employees earn $11.50 per hour or less) offered health insurance to their employees in 2010, while about 90 percent of employers with 100 to 999 employees who earn low wages did.

To provide an incentive for small employers to provide health insurance, and to make insurance more affordable, Congress included the Small Employer Health Insurance Tax Credit (referred to in this chapter as the credit) in the Patient Protection and Affordable Care Act (PPACA).[2] The credit is available for tax years beginning after December 31, 2009 to certain employers with employees earning low wages— small business and tax-exempt entities—that pay at least half of their employees' health insurance premiums. The Congressional Budget Office (CBO) and the Joint Committee on Taxation (JCT) jointly estimated that the credit would cost $2 billion in fiscal year 2010 and $40 billion from fiscal years 2010 to 2019.[3]

You asked us to review the implementation of the credit. Specifically, we examined

- to what extent the credit is being claimed and what factors, if any, limit employer claims, and how these factors can be addressed;
- how fully the Internal Revenue Service (IRS) is ensuring that the credit is correctly claimed by eligible employers; and
- what data are needed to evaluate the effects of the credit.

To describe the extent to which the credit is being claimed, we reviewed IRS data on the claims for tax year 2010. To identify any factors that may limit credit claims and to assess how they could be addressed, we interviewed IRS officials as well as groups representing employers, tax preparers, and insurance brokers, and worked with them to assemble discussion groups on the credit. To assess how these factors could be addressed, we analyzed our interview results as well as relevant documents. Where possible, we identified IRS or MEPS data related to the factors. To assess how IRS is ensuring that the tax credit is correctly claimed by eligible employers we reviewed its compliance plans for the credit and compared them to practices used successfully for prior tax provisions[4] and IRS strategic objectives. We interviewed IRS officials on their compliance efforts. To assess what data would be needed to evaluate the effects of the credit, we conducted a literature review and interviewed interest groups and subject matter specialists from government, academia, research foundations and think tanks. We found the data we used to be sufficiently reliable for the purposes of our report.

We conducted this performance audit from July 2011 through May 2012 in accordance with generally accepted government auditing standards. Those standards require that we plan and perform the audit to obtain sufficient, appropriate evidence to provide a reasonable basis for our findings and conclusions based on our audit objectives. We believe that the evidence obtained provides a reasonable basis for our findings and conclusions based on our audit objectives. (See app. I for our scope and methodology.)

BACKGROUND

Small Employer Health Insurance Market

Small employers with low-wage employees do not commonly offer health insurance, compared with large employers with low-wage employees, as shown in figure 1.

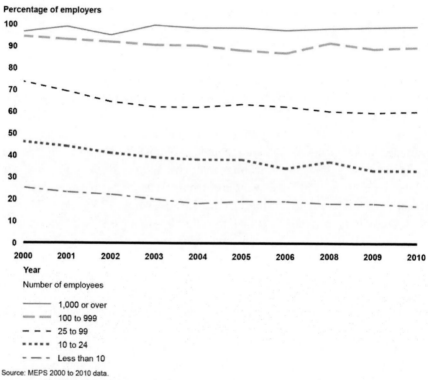

Percentage of employers

Year

Number of employees

——— 1,000 or over
— — 100 to 999
— — — 25 to 99
▪ ▪ ▪ ▪ ▪ 10 to 24
- — - Less than 10

Source: MEPS 2000 to 2010 data.

Notes: Figure includes for-profit and nonprofit (tax-exempt) entities but not government entities. A low-wage employer is defined as an employer that has 50 percent or more of its employees earning a low wage (earning $11.50 per hour or less, which is an annual salary of, at most, about $23,920). Data were not collected for the MEPS Insurance Component for 2007.

Figure 1. Percentage of Employers with Low-Wage Employees That Offer Health Insurance, 2000 through 2010, by Employer Size.

A combination of factors explains why small, low-wage employers tend not to offer health insurance.[5]

- For very low-wage employees, such as minimum wage employees,[6] health insurance drives up total compensation costs for employees.
- Low-wage employees working for small employers generally prefer to receive wages over insurance benefits as part of total compensation. On one hand, while employees pay both income and employment tax on wages, employees do not have to pay income or employment taxes on premiums paid by their employers for health insurance. However, for low-wage employees, the income tax exclusion is worth less relative to cash wages than for higher-income employees because low-wage employees may be in a lower income tax bracket.[7]
- Insurers of small employers face higher per-employee fixed costs for billing and marketing[8] and are less able to pool risk[9] across large numbers of employees. As a result, plans offered to small employers are likely to have higher premiums or have less coverage and higher out-of-pocket costs than plans offered to large employers.[10]

IRS Implementation and Requirements for Calculating and Claiming the Credit

IRS's Small Business and Self-Employed Division (SB/SE) and Tax Exempt and Government Entities Division (TEGE) are primarily responsible for implementing the credit. IRS works with the Department of Health and Human Services (HHS) and the Small Business Administration (SBA) on implementation tasks, such as outreach and communication.

To be eligible, an employer must:

- Be a small business[11] or tax-exempt employer[12] located in or having trade or business income in the United States and pay premiums for employee health insurance coverage issued in the United States.
- Employ fewer than 25 full-time-equivalent (FTE)[13] employees in the tax year (excluding certain employees, such as business owners and their family members).[14]

- Pay average annual wages of less than $50,000 per FTE in the tax year.[15]
- Offer health insurance and pay at least 50 percent of the health insurance premium under a "qualifying arrangement." This means that the employer uniformly pays at least 50 percent of the cost of premiums for enrolled employees, although IRS did develop relaxed criteria for meeting this requirement for tax year 2010.[16]

The President's fiscal year 2013 budget request contains a proposal for expanding the credit's eligibility criteria to include employers with 50 or fewer FTEs and removing the uniform contribution requirement.

Limits on the Credit Amount

The amount of the credit that employers can claim depends on several factors. Through 2013, small businesses can receive up to 35 percent and tax-exempt entities can receive up to 25 percent of their base payments for employee health insurance premiums; these portions rise to 50 percent and 35 percent, respectively, starting in 2014. Employers can receive the full credit percentage if they have 10 or fewer FTEs and pay an average of $25,000 or less in annual wages; employers with 11 to 25 FTEs and average wages exceeding $25,000 up to $50,000 are eligible for a partial credit that "phases" out to zero percent of premium payments as the FTE and wage amounts rise. Figure 2 shows the phaseout of the credit for small businesses; the phaseout for tax-exempt entities follows a similar pattern, up to 25 percent of health insurance premiums.

Further, the amount of the credit is limited if the premiums paid by an employer are more than the average premiums determined by HHS for the small group market in the state in which the employer offers insurance. The credit percentage is multiplied by the allowable premium to calculate the dollar amount of credit claimed. For example, in Alabama, the state average premium was $4,441 for a single employee in 2010. If an employer claiming the credit in Alabama paid $5,000 for a single employee's health premium, the credit would be calculated using the state average premium of $4,441 rather than the actual premium paid. Appendix II shows the average premiums by state.

The proposal in the President's Budget suggests beginning the phaseout at 21 FTEs, rather than 11, as well as providing for a more gradual combined phaseout for the credit percentages and removing the state market limits.

Average wage

Number of FTEs	$25,000 and less	$30,000	$35,000	$40,000	$45,000	$50,000
10 and fewer	35%	28%	21%	14%	7%	0%
11	33%	26%	19%	12%	5%	0%
12	30%	23%	16%	9%	2%	0%
13	28%	21%	14%	7%	0%	0%
14	26%	19%	12%	5%	0%	0%
15	23%	16%	9%	2%	0%	0%
16	21%	14%	7%	0%	0%	0%
17	19%	12%	5%	0%	0%	0%
18	16%	9%	2%	0%	0%	0%
19	14%	7%	0%	0%	0%	0%
20	12%	5%	0%	0%	0%	0%
21	9%	2%	0%	0%	0%	0%
22	7%	0%	0%	0%	0%	0%
23	5%	0%	0%	0%	0%	0%
24	2%	0%	0%	0%	0%	0%
25	0%	0%	0%	0%	0%	0%

Source: Congressional Research Service.

Note: GAO adapted the graphic from Congressional Research Service, *Summary of the Small Business Health Insurance Tax Credit Under PPACA (P.L. 111-148)* (Washington, D.C.: Apr. 5, 2010).

Figure 2. Phaseout of the Credit for Small Businesses as a Percentage of Employer Contributions to Premiums, for 2010 to 2013.

Process for Claiming the Credit

Employers are to calculate the credit amount on IRS Form 8941, "Credit for Small Employer Health Insurance Premiums." Small businesses are to claim the credit as part of the general business tax credit (on Form 3800), and use it to offset actual tax liability. If they do not have a federal tax liability, they cannot receive the credit as a refund but may carry the credit forward or back to offset tax liabilities for other years.[17] Credit amounts claimed by partnerships and S corporations are to be passed through to their partners and shareholders, respectively,[18] who may claim their portions of the credit on their individual income tax returns.[19] Tax-exempt entities are to claim the credit on Form 990-T, "Exempt Organization Business Income Tax Return," and receive the credit as a refund even though the employer has no taxable income.

Employers that claim the credit can also deduct health insurance expenses on their tax returns but must subtract the amount of the credit from the deduction. Employers can claim the credit for up to 6 years—the initial 4 years from 2010 through 2013 and any 2 consecutive years after 2013 if they buy insurance through the Small Business Health Option Programs, which are part of the insurance exchanges to be established under PPACA.[20]

FEWER SMALL EMPLOYERS CLAIMED THE CREDIT THAN WERE THOUGHT TO BE ELIGIBLE BECAUSE OF FACTORS SUCH AS CREDIT SIZE AND COMPLEXITY

Actual Credit Claims Were Much Lower Than Initial Rough Eligibility Estimates

Fewer small employers claimed the credit for tax year 2010 than were thought to be eligible based on rough estimates of eligible employers made by government agencies and small business groups. IRS data on total claimants, adjusted to account for claims by partners and shareholders, show that about 170,300 small employers made claims for the credit in 2010.[21] (See app. III for adjustments to determine claims filed by employers.) The average credit amount claimed was about $2,700. Limited information is available on the distribution of claim amounts for business entities because IRS focuses its data collection on the taxpayers filing credit claims, who may be partners or shareholders claiming their portions of a business entity's credit. Appendix III provides additional detail.

Selected estimates, made by government agencies and small business groups, of employers eligible for the credit range from around 1.4 million to 4 million. However, data limitations mean that these estimates are necessarily rough. Based on our review of available data sources on the three basic eligibility rules for the credit—involving wages, FTEs, and health insurance—it is not possible to combine data from various sources to closely match these rules. (See app. VI for details.) Though statistical modeling corrects for imperfect data to match these rules, models are not precise. While acknowledging the data limitations, several entities produced estimates of the number of employers potentially eligible for the credit. The Council of Economic Advisors estimated 4 million and SBA estimated 2.6 million.[22] Other groups making estimates included small business groups such as the Small Business Majority (SBM) and the National Federation of Independent Businesses (NFIB). Their estimates were 4 million and 1.4 million, respectively.[23]

A similar pattern is seen when the dollar value of credits actually claimed is compared to initial estimates. The dollar value of claims made in 2010 was $468 million compared to initial cost estimates of $2 billion for 2010 (a CBO and JCT joint estimate).[24]

Most Small Employer Claims Were Reduced Because of the Phaseout Rules and Some Were Reduced by the State Average Premiums

Most of the claims were for less than the full credit percentage. Of the approximately 170,300 small employers making claims for tax year 2010, 142,200—83 percent—could not use the full credit percentage. Usually employers could not meet the average wage requirement to claim the full percentage, as about 68 percent did not qualify based on wages but did meet the FTE requirement. (See figure 3.)[25]

State average premiums also reduced some credit amounts by reducing the amount of the premium base against which the credit percentage is applied. This premium base may be reduced when it exceeds the state average premiums for small group plans,[26] as determined by HHS. If so, small employers are to use the state average amount, which in essence caps the premium amount used to calculate their credit. According to IRS data, this cap reduced the credit for around 30 percent of employer claims. For example, a nonprofit representative told us that her credit dropped from $7,900 to $3,070 because of the cap in her state. (See app. II for small group average premiums in all states.)

Credit Phaseout

(In reference to the phaseout) "People get excited that they're eligible and then they do the calculations and it's like the bottom just falls out of it and it's not really there. It's almost like a wish that they might get it and then they do the calculations and it's not worth it for them." –Health insurance discussion group participant

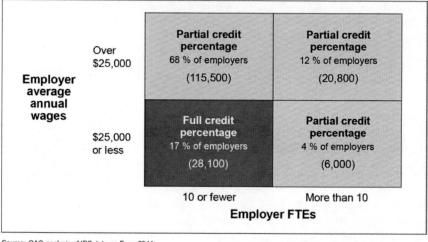

Source: GAO analysis of IRS data on Form 8941.

Notes: This information is based on the approximately 170,300 small employer claims. Numbers are rounded to the nearest hundred. Numbers and percentages do not add to totals because of rounding.

Figure 3. Percentage and Number of Small Employers Claiming the Full and Partial Credit Percentages, by FTE and Wage Requirements for the Credit, Tax Year 2010.

State Averages as Caps on the Credit

"I don't know where that number (the state average) comes from but that's supposed to be the average cost, and that seems pretty low, which is reducing that tax credit amount they would qualify for." –Health insurance discussion group participant

Most Small Employers Could Not Meet the Health Insurance Requirement for the Credit and the Credit Was Not Seen as an Incentive to Start Offering Insurance

Small, Low-Wage Employers Not Commonly Offering Health Insurance

"Very few people are going to pay 50 or 100 percent of the health insurance for someone making $25,000 or less. We just don't have that many clients who even start to qualify." –Tax preparer discussion group participant

As already discussed, small employers do not commonly offer health insurance. MEPS estimates that 83 percent of employers who may otherwise be eligible for the full credit[27] did not offer health insurance in 2010 and that 67 percent of employers who could be eligible for the partial credit[28] did not offer insurance. Our discussion groups and other interviewees confirmed this, with comments and examples of small, low-wage employers not offering health insurance to employees.

Furthermore, the small employers do not likely view the credit as a big enough incentive to begin offering health insurance and to make a credit claim, according to employer representatives, tax preparers, and insurance brokers we met with. While some small employers could be eligible for the credit if they began to offer health insurance, small business group representatives and discussion group participants told us that the credit may not offset costs enough to justify a new outlay for health insurance premiums. Related to this concern, the credit being available for 6 years overall and just 2 consecutive years after 2014 further detracts from any potential incentive to small employers to start offering health insurance in order to claim the credit.

Complexity Deterred Small Employer Claims, According to Discussion Groups

Complexity of the Credit

"Any credit that needs a form that takes 25 lines and seven work sheets to build to those 25 lines is too complicated." –Tax preparer discussion group participant.

Most discussion group participants and groups we interviewed found the tax credit to be complicated, deterring small employers from claiming it. The complexity arises from the various eligibility requirements, the various data that must be recorded and collected, and number of worksheets to be completed.

A major complaint we heard centered on gathering information for and calculating FTEs and the health insurance premiums associated with those FTEs. Eligible employers reportedly did not have the number of hours worked for each employee readily available to calculate FTEs and their associated average annual wages nor did they have the required health insurance information for each employee readily available.

Gathering Information for the Credit Calculation

(Small business owners) "Are trying to run their businesses and operate and make a profit, and when you tell them they need to take 2, 3, 4 hours to gather this information, they just shake their head and say, 'no, I'm not going to do it'."–Tax preparer discussion group participant

Exclusions from the definition of "employee" and other rules make the calculations complex. For example, seasonal employees are excluded from FTE counts but insurance premiums paid on their behalf count toward the employer's credit. Incorporating the phaseout also complicates the credit calculation.

In our discussion groups with tax preparers, we heard that small business owners generally do not want to spend the time or money to gather the necessary information to calculate the credit, given that the credit will likely be insubstantial. Tax preparers told us it could take their clients from 2 to 8 hours or possibly longer to gather the necessary information to calculate the credit and that the tax preparers spent, in general, 3 to 5 hours calculating the credit.[29] We did hear from a couple of participants— a small business owner and a nonprofit representative—that they did not find the credit overly burdensome.

Tax preparers we interviewed said that IRS did the best it could with the Form 8941 given the credit's complexity. IRS officials said they did not receive criticism about Form 8941 itself but did hear that the instructions and its seven worksheets were too long and cumbersome for some claimants and tax preparers. On its website, IRS tried to reduce the burden on taxpayers by offering "3 Simple Steps" as a screening tool to help taxpayers determine whether they might be eligible for the credit. However, to calculate the actual dollars that can be claimed, the three steps become 15 calculations, 11 of which are based on seven worksheets, some of which request multiple columns of information. Figure 4 shows IRS's "3 Simple Steps," for Form 8941. (See app. V for full text for this figure.)

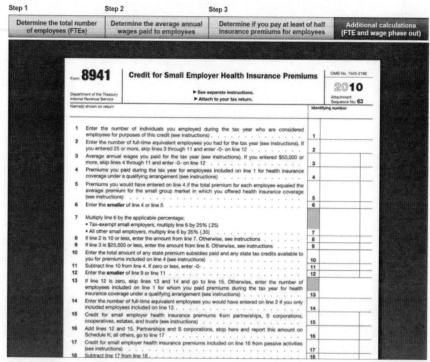

Source: GAO analysis of IRS information.

To view worksheets included in this graphic, go to appendix V.

Figure 4. Form 8941 and IRS's "3 Simple Steps" for Determining Potential Eligibility.

Given the effort involved to make a claim and the uncertainty about the credit amounts, a few discussion group participants said it would be helpful to be able to quickly estimate employers' eligibility for the credit and the amount they might receive; this would help them to decide whether the credit would be worth the effort, although this would not reduce the complication of filing out Form 8941 because, to fill out the form, full documentation would need to be reviewed. IRS's Taxpayer Advocate Service[30] is developing a calculator for IRS's website to quickly estimate an employer's eligibility, but this will still require gathering information such as wages, FTEs, and insurance plans. We also heard concerns that a calculator could cause confusion for clients who find they are eligible when quickly estimating the credit but then turn out to be ineligible or find they are eligible for a smaller credit when their accountant fills out Form 8941.

The Extent to Which Lack of Awareness Is a Factor Limiting More Claims Is Unknown, Although IRS Did Significant Outreach

Many small businesses reported that they were unaware of the credit. The NFIB Research Foundation[31] and the Kaiser Family Foundation both estimated that approximately 50 percent of small businesses were aware of the credit, as of May 2011, or more than 1 year after Congress authorized this credit.[32]

The extent to which being unaware prevented eligible employers from claiming the credit for tax year 2010 is not known. Some discussion group participants raised concerns about unawareness, but they also cited other factors limiting credit claims for tax year 2010. If 50 percent of small businesses knew about the credit, then the approximately 170,300 claims is a relatively small proportion of those that were knowledgeable. This indicates that other factors contributed to employers not claiming the credit. Further, it is hard to interpret the impact of awareness on claims because these surveys included an unknown number of small business employers that would not be eligible for the credit regardless of their awareness. For those employers that were unaware, the surveys did not account for their accountants or tax preparers that may have known about the credit but did not tell their clients about it because they did not believe their clients would qualify or because the credit amount would be very small. In addition, the surveys did not cover tax-exempt entities.

To raise awareness of the credit, IRS did significant outreach. IRS developed a communication and outreach plan, written materials on the credit, a video, and a website. IRS officials also reached out to interest groups about the credit and developed a list of target audiences and presentation topics. IRS officials began speaking at events in April 2010 to discuss the credit and attended over 1,500 in-person or web-based events from April 2010 to February 2012. Discussion of the credit at the events varied from being a portion of a presentation covering many topics to some events that focused on the credit with a dedicated discussion period.

IRS does not know whether its outreach efforts actually increased awareness of the credit or were otherwise cost-effective. It would be challenging to estimate the impact of IRS's outreach efforts on awareness with a rigorous methodology; however, based on ongoing feedback they received from interest groups, IRS officials told us they believe their efforts have been worthwhile. IRS used some feedback from focus groups of tax preparers and from other sources[33] to revise its outreach efforts. For example, IRS modified its outreach from initially focusing on tax preparers and small employers to including insurance brokers in 2012.

Addressing Factors and Expanding Credit Use May Require Substantive Design Changes

Given that most small employers do not offer insurance and what we heard about the size of the credit not being big enough to incentivize offering health insurance,[34] it may not be possible to significantly expand credit use without changing the credit's eligibility. Most claims were for partial credits and many people we spoke with view the credit amount as too small and temporary to justify providing health insurance when none is provided now. In addition, given that IRS has conducted extensive outreach about the credit, it is not likely that more outreach would significantly increase the number of businesses claiming the credit. Amending the eligibility requirements or increasing the amount of the credit may allow more businesses to take advantage of the credit,[35] but these changes would increase its cost to the Federal government. Options include the following:

- Increasing the amount of the full credit, the partial credit, or both.
- Increasing the amount of the credit for some by eliminating state premium averages.
- Expanding eligibility requirements by increasing the number of FTEs and wage limit allowable for employers to claim the partial credit, the full credit, or both. This expansion would not, however, likely affect the smallest employers which do not offer health insurance.
- Simplifying the calculation of the credit in the following ways:
  - Using the number of employees and wage information already reported on the employer's tax return. This could reduce the amount of data gathering as well as credit calculations because eligibility would be based on the number of employees and not FTEs. A trade-off with this option would be less precision in targeting the full and partial credit amount to specific small employer subgroups.[36]

- Offering a flat credit amount per FTE (or number of employees) rather than a percentage, which would reduce the precision in targeting the credit.

The data limitations that made it difficult to estimate the number of businesses eligible for the current credit also make it difficult to estimate the impact of any design changes.

IRS IS IMPLEMENTING SEVERAL PRACTICES FROM PRIOR COMPLIANCE EFFORTS, BUT ADDITIONAL STEPS COULD BE TAKEN

IRS Incorporated Practices from Strategic Objectives and Prior Compliance Efforts

IRS's compliance efforts for the credit incorporate practices that have been shown effective in helping to ensure compliance with other tax provisions or are consistent with IRS strategic objectives. Some of those practices were used for the Telephone Excise Tax Refund (TETR)[37] and Consolidated Omnibus Budget Reconciliation Act (COBRA) subsidies for health insurance for the unemployed, according to IRS officials.[38] Specifically, IRS is doing the following:

- Using computerized filters to review credit claims on Forms 8941 for certain errors or potential problems that may trigger an examination of the claim.
- Transcribing more lines of data from Form 8941 into IRS computer systems which should make the filters more effective. Although transcribing more lines increases processing and data storage costs, IRS plans to transcribe more lines for tax years 2011 and 2012 claims to ensure better verification of eligibility.
- Freezing refunds of tax-exempt entities whose returns have been selected for examination, which avoids the costs of trying to recover funds.[39]
- Considering the documentation burden on claimants. IRS did not require claimants to submit documentation on health insurance

premiums with their Form 8941 because IRS officials said they will review examination results and may revisit the decision not to require documentation if results suggest that such documentation would improve compliance checks.

- Modifying filters, as needed, in response to observed trends. For example, a filter that applies to tax-exempt organization claims was tripped by about a quarter of claimant organizations, as of December 31, 2011. IRS officials said some eligible tax-exempt entities tripped the filter because it was too broad. To address this, IRS modified the filter to more clearly identify qualifying tax-exempt organizations.

- Completing a risk assessment on compliance issues related to the credit. The assessment identified risks involving refunds for tax-exempt entities, difficulties verifying employment tax return information for certain employers, and not using existing Math Error Authority (MEA).

- Considering the costs and benefits of MEA for the credit.[40] IRS officials identified three filters whose type of errors could be addressed with MEA. They noted that less than 1 percent of Forms 8941 tripped one or more of those filters,[41] which IRS officials said does not justify the costs to develop procedures to use MEA, if it were granted.[42]

Filters Check Some Eligibility Criteria, but Are Limited by Available Data

IRS developed 21 filters for Form 8941, some of which apply differently to SB/SE and TEGE taxpayers. The filters cover some of the eligibility requirements for the credit. Errors on about 3.5 percent (11,763) of Forms 8941 for tax year 2010 tripped 1 or more filters; almost half of those forms were from tax-exempt entities. According to IRS officials, the filter failure rate is consistent with other recent tax credits.

The filters do not cover all of the credit's requirements for several data-related reasons.[43] In one case, data are not included on Form 8941 but may be included on worksheets required to be retained by claimants (e.g., information on business owner family members or seasonal employees included in credit calculations); in another case, certain data are not transcribed (e.g., the credit amount for certain claimants). For other requirements, IRS officials stated that reasonable filters cannot easily be developed because of challenges with matching data.

Some Form 8941 filters also face limitations mainly because of problems with data or IRS's systems.

- Filters are mutually exclusive, meaning that filters on related requirements are viewed in isolation. However, according to IRS officials, IRS has ways to identify whether a form failed more than one filter, which IRS considers when identifying returns for potential examination.
- Some filters may mistakenly target eligible claimants because the filters rely on general thresholds in Form 8941 data or, in some cases, other IRS data (such as employee-level data) that are not exact matches to data on the Form 8941.

Data on Forms W-2 (employees' annual Wage and Tax Statement) could provide additional data for filters once the provision in PPACA is implemented that requires employers to report the cost—including both employer and employee contributions—of certain types of health insurance provided to an employee.[44] IRS officials said the data have limited use because, among other things, they would not provide details for determining whether an employer met the credit's requirements for health insurance; therefore, IRS officials will not pursue using the data at this time. Nevertheless, the data could be used in a filter to identify claimants who reported no health insurance contributions on Form W-2 and therefore may not be offering health insurance. In the absence of other documentation or third-party reporting on health insurance, using Form W-2 data in a filter could be a cost-effective, rough indicator of whether a claimant is paying employee health insurance premiums, without increasing taxpayer burden. However, IRS provided transition relief to employers that file fewer than 250 Forms W-2 per year, and issued guidance stating that these employers will not be required to report the data until further guidance is issued. As a result, it is unlikely that the data could be useful before 2014, the year when the credit will only be available to employers for any 2 consecutive years.

Examination Instructions Cover Most Eligibility Requirements, but Gaps Exist

After the filters are run, IRS creates lists of claims to consider for further examination. SB/SE wanted enough examination cases to spot check different filters and claims from different regions, to enable them to establish a field presence and to learn about compliance risks with the credit, according to an SB/SE official.[45] Examination staff in SB/SE and TEGE are to follow a set of instructions when doing examinations.[46]

SB/SE's examination instructions address all of the credit's requirements for small businesses to claim the credit except that they do not include specific instructions for examiners on determining eligibility of claimants with non-U.S. addresses. An employer located outside of the United States with a business or trade interest in the United States may claim the credit only if the employer pays premiums for coverage issued in and regulated by one of the states or the District of Columbia. Without a prompt in examination instructions, IRS examiners may overlook claimants that do not comply with the address requirements. An SB/SE official said IRS has no instructions for examiners to review claimants with non-U.S. addresses during an examination on the credit because potential compliance problems with businesses with non-U.S. addresses exist for other tax credits. This, however, was not IRS's approach for another general business tax issue relevant to the credit—whether claimants that carry back the credit to offset tax liabilities in previous years did so properly. Near the end of our work, SB/SE added guidance to one of its examination instruction documents to cover the carry back issue.

Instructions for TEGE examiners also address most of the eligibility requirements to claim the credits, but, like SB/SE's, TEGE examination instructions do not address how to review claimants with non-U.S. addresses.[47] Further, TEGE instructions for some of the credit's requirements have less detail compared to SB/SE's instructions. TEGE's instructions provide steps on how to determine if an employer's insurance premiums paid met "qualifying arrangement" and other criteria, but they provide less detail than SB/SE instructions. For example, SB/SE guidance instructs examiners to review health insurance policies and invoices to confirm premium payments, and to review other documentation to check whether the employer offers health benefits that are not eligible for the credit. TEGE instructions do not suggest these steps and also do not provide a prompt for examiners to ensure that insurance premiums paid on behalf of seasonal employees are included in calculations.

According to IRS officials, the TEGE examiners are trained specifically for doing examinations on the credit and therefore need less guidance than SB/SE examiners, who work on multiple issues simultaneously. However, TEGE examination documents contain detailed guidance in a workbook format for these trained examiners on other credit requirements. Without detailed guidance for TEGE examiners that instructs them on how to examine health insurance documents, examiners may not consistently identify noncompliance, which could lead to erroneous credit refunds. This could particularly be the case as examining health insurance documents to check eligibility for this new credit has not been typical work for these examiners.

Examinations Under Way, but IRS Needs to Develop a Plan for Efficiently Analyzing Results on Credit Compliance

For tax year 2010, SB/SE plans to conduct over 1,500 examinations related to the credit, and TEGE anticipates about 1,000 examinations. An SB/SE official said the number of examinations is expected to provide initial compliance information and allow IRS to establish a compliance presence without committing too many resources initially. TEGE selected its number of examinations based on resource decisions, before tax year 2010 claims began. Neither SB/SE nor TEGE adjusted the number of examinations once actual claim numbers were known. As a result, the percentage of TEGE claims being examined is high, according to a TEGE official. Table 1 summarizes the status of IRS's examinations on the credit.

IRS's database on examination results tracks the aggregate dollar amount of tax changes as a result of the examination but does not contain the reason a change is made. Consequently, IRS is not able to isolate and analyze examination results related to the credit versus other tax issues. This is particularly a problem for SB/SE examinations, which may cover issues other than the credit.[48] Instead, as initial examinations have closed, IRS officials said that management has spoken with examiners about findings related to the credit. This has been possible because of the relatively low initial volume of cases, but this approach may not be feasible as results accumulate. Therefore, it is not clear how IRS can efficiently analyze results to decide whether changes are necessary in how it examines the credit or how it educates small employers about how to comply with the credit's rules, and whether it committed too many or too few resources to examinations of the credit.

Table 1. Examination Actions for Form 8941 as of February 2012, for Tax Year 2010

Number of:	SB/SE[a]	TEGE	Total
Examinations initiated	500	570	**1,070**
Additional examinations anticipated	1,000	430	**1,430**
Closed examinations	119	88	**207**
Closed examinations resulting in a change to the credit amount	46	22	**68**

Sources: SB/SE and TEGE officials.

[a] For examinations, SB/SE does not distinguish between examinations on business or individual claimants.

Furthermore, IRS does not have criteria for deciding whether the resources spent on examinations of the credit are appropriate, given the amount of errors found. IRS officials said that for future years they plan to select the number of credit examinations based on past results, identified compliance risks, and available resources. However, without criteria to assess the results in concert with these risks and resources, IRS is less able to ensure that examination resources target errors with the credit, rather than examining compliant claimants.

For example, early examination results (as of February 2012) show that 67 percent of the examinations completed were closed without changing the credit amount. Examinations without a change burden taxpayers and use IRS resources. We recognize that few of the planned examinations have been completed and the "no change" percentage could change. According to IRS officials, cases resulting in "no change" tend to be the first cases closed because they close more quickly than cases requiring a change. However, IRS is not using change rate information from prior tax credits to determine if examinations for the credit have a "high" no-change rate, which could be one indicator to help decide how many examination resources to apply to the credit. IRS officials said they do not plan to use data from examinations of other tax provisions to benchmark measures— such as the no-change rate or length of time an examination is open— because results would not be comparable.

A summary of examination results specific to the credit could also inform decisions about using additional compliance tools such as soft notices.[49] In the past, IRS has used soft notices to correct errors and collect funds without initiating an examination.[50] A senior IRS official who is implementing the credit said IRS has not ruled out using soft notices, but examination results would need to identify an issue that would justify their use. He said soft notices are not effective for all taxpayers or situations. He said IRS would consider using soft notices if officials found a series of returns with mistakes from the same tax preparer or promoter of tax schemes. Furthermore, soft notices may necessitate follow-up, which would negate some of the advantages of the notices. If IRS analysis showed that examinations were not a cost-effective way to pursue certain errors made in claiming a credit, a soft notice may offer another approach to improving compliance with lower costs to IRS and less burden on claimants.

DATA TO EVALUATE MANY QUESTIONS ABOUT THE EFFECTS OF THE CREDIT ARE NOT AVAILABLE

There are a variety of research questions that could be of interest to policymakers about the effects of the credit that cannot be evaluated with data currently available. Figure 5 shows how the credit may influence employer behavior and, ultimately, employees.

To answer research questions about the credits potential outcomes shown in figure 5, the following are examples of data that might be needed:

- number of small, low-wage employers offering health insurance, before and after the credit was available;
- number of employees at small, low-wage employers, who have or could obtain health insurance through their employers; and
- amount of annual health insurance premium costs for small, low-wage employers before and after the credit.

None of these data are readily available or free of limitations, which complicates an evaluation. For example, the available data on employer-sponsored health insurance do not align with the credit's eligibility criteria, according to our interviews with subject matter specialists and our review of the data (see app. VI for a summary of the data sources), nor could we identify a data source that tracks when, and why, employers begin offering insurance. As a result of the limitations with all three types of data, it would be difficult to precisely measure changes in health insurance availability, offering, and costs because of the credit, without collecting additional data. Isolating influential factors—such as those shown in figure 5—that may contribute to the effects of the credit would also be a challenge in an evaluation.[51]

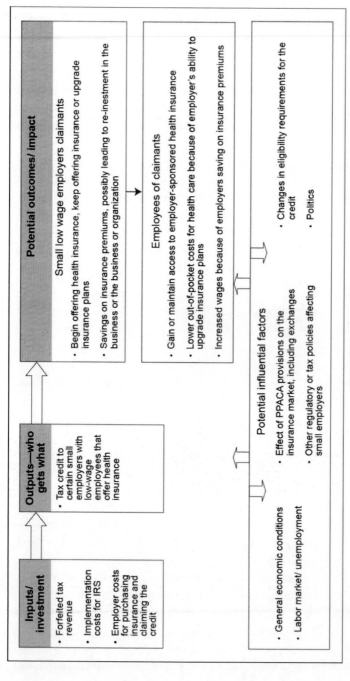

Note: Basic model structure is based on University of Wisconsin Extension Program Development and Evaluation model, as shown in GAO-12-208G. Content and relationships among variables are based on GAO analysis of interviews with subject matter specialists, and literature review.

Figure 5. Model of Potential Outcomes and Influential Factors for the Small Employer Health Insurance Tax Credit.

IRS officials said they will not collect data on credit claimants, outside of those collected on Form 8941. IRS's position on data collection for all provisions of the tax code is that it only collects data it needs to ensure compliance with the tax laws.[52]

Collecting additional data needed for policy evaluation would have costs, and the magnitude of those costs would depend on the type and amount of data needed, which depends on the research questions being asked. An additional consideration in thinking about the benefits and costs of additional data collection for policy evaluation purposes is the time limits on claiming the credit. The current version of the credit runs through the end of 2014.[53] Policymakers' conclusions about the questions to be answered by any evaluations of the credit's effects would determine the type of data that would need to be collected.

CONCLUSIONS

The Small Employer Health Insurance Tax Credit was intended to offer an incentive for small, low-wage employers to provide health insurance. However, utilization of the credit has been lower than expected, with the available evidence suggesting that the design of the credit is a large part of the reason why. While the credit could be redesigned, such changes come with trade-offs. Changing the credit to expand eligibility or make it more generous would increase the revenue loss to the federal government.

In administering the credit to ensure compliance, IRS employed a number of practices that were shown effective for other tax provisions or are consistent with IRS strategic objectives. Nevertheless, we identified several opportunities for IRS to either improve compliance or perhaps reduce the resources it is devoting to ensuring compliance. Without additional guidance for examiners on employers with non-U.S. addresses, there is a risk of improper credit claims being allowed. Without more systematic attention to early examination results, IRS could lock itself into devoting more scarce resources than needed to examinations.

RECOMMENDATIONS FOR EXECUTIVE ACTION

To help ensure thoroughness and consistency of examinations on the credit, we recommend that the Commissioner of Internal Revenue take the following two actions:

1. Revise the SB/SE and TEGE examination instructions to include instructions for examiners on how to confirm eligibility for the credit for small employers with non-U.S. addresses.
2. Revise the TEGE examination guidance to include more detailed instructions for examiners on how to confirm that claimants properly calculated eligible health insurance premiums paid for purposes of the credit. The SB/SE examination instructions could serve as a model.

To help ensure that IRS uses its examination resources efficiently, we recommend that the Commissioner of Internal Revenue take the following two actions:

3. Document and analyze the results of examinations involving the credit to identify how much of those results are related to the credit versus other tax issues being examined, what errors are being made in claiming the credit, and when the examinations of the credit are worth the resource investment.
4. Related to the above analysis of examination results on the credit, identify the types of errors with the credit that could be addressed with alternative approaches, such as soft notices.

AGENCY COMMENTS AND OUR EVALUATION

In an April 30, 2012, letter responding to a draft of this chapter the IRS Deputy Commissioner for Services and Enforcement provided comments on our findings and recommendations as well as information on additional agency efforts related to implementing the Small Employer Health Insurance Tax Credit in PPACA. IRS generally agreed with all four of our recommendations. Regarding our recommendation on examination instructions related to small employers with non-U.S. addresses, IRS stated that SB/SE will provide additional guidance in its instructions and that TEGE has added guidance to its instructions. On May 1, 2012, IRS provided a copy of the TEGE instructions, which we are reviewing. On our recommendation on revising TEGE's examination guidance, IRS's letter said that on April 13, 2012, TEGE implemented more detailed instructions in its examination guidance related to confirming proper calculations of eligible health insurance premiums paid for purposes of the credit. These instructions were also included in the TEGE document provided on May 1, 2012.

With regard to analyzing credit examination results to identify compliance issues specific to the credit, IRS said it regularly analyzes audit results to determine whether resources are expended efficiently, though its information systems do not currently capture adjustments by issue, such as this tax credit. IRS agreed to leverage existing information systems and, as appropriate, to allocate resources to manually analyze examination results. IRS said this will include, as feasible, identifying the types and amounts of errors related to the credit. We reiterate the benefit of documenting and analyzing the results of examinations involving the credit. If it does not do so, IRS will not have information for determining whether examinations of the credit are worth the resource investment.

Regarding our fourth recommendation on using examination results to determine whether alternative compliance approaches, such as soft notices, could help address errors with the credit, IRS agreed to continue to review its compliance efforts to determine whether soft notices would be appropriate.

James R. White
Director, Tax Issues
Strategic Issues

APPENDIX I. SCOPE AND METHODOLOGY

To assess the extent to which the Small Employer Health Insurance Tax Credit (referred to in this chapter as the credit) is being claimed, we obtained and analyzed Internal Revenue Service (IRS) data on the claims on Form 8941 for tax year 2010. We interviewed responsible IRS staff and examined background materials. IRS provided a report from the Form 8941 data and we reviewed the programming code that created that report. We corroborated the results of this IRS report with a Treasury Inspector General for Tax Administration (TIGTA) report published in November and found similarities.[54] The data were found to be sufficiently reliable for our purposes. We identified estimates of employers that were potentially eligible to claim the credit by reviewing reports and websites of government agencies, think tanks, and interest groups. When possible, we interviewed officials from the government agencies and business groups that developed estimates.

To identify any factors limiting credit claims, we interviewed groups representing employers, tax preparers and insurance brokers and to assess how these factors could be addressed, we analyzed our interview results as well as relevant documents. Specifically, we spoke with representatives of the National Federation of Independent Businesses, the National Council of Nonprofits, the Small Business Majority, the U.S. Chamber of Commerce, the American Institute of Certified Public Accountants, America's Health Insurance Plans, the National Society of Accountants, the National Association of Enrolled Agents, and the National Association of Health Underwriters. We worked with some of these groups to assemble discussion groups with tax preparers, health insurance brokers, and employers to discuss potential factors and ways to address them. Discussion groups were, for the most part, telephone conferences. We also spoke with insurance and tax preparation companies, specifically, BlueCross Blue Shield of Kansas City, Independent Health of New York, H&R Block's Tax Institute, and Jackson Hewitt Tax Service. We used qualitative analysis software to do a content analysis of the interviews and discussion group comments.

To provide additional support for discussion group and interview findings we reviewed documents and, where possible, we identified data from IRS, the 2010 Medical Expenditure Panel Survey, or the 2011 Kaiser Family Foundation Health Benefits Survey. At IRS, we interviewed officials from the Small Business/Self-Employed Division (SB/SE), including officials in the Communications and Liaison Office; the Tax Exempt and Government Entities Division (TEGE); the Research and Analysis for Tax Administration division, and the Taxpayer Advocacy Service.

To assess how fully IRS is ensuring that the tax credit is correctly claimed by eligible employers, we reviewed IRS's compliance plan and filters and instructions for IRS staff conducting examinations, and compared these documents with compliance practices used for prior tax provisions and found in IRS strategic objectives.[55] We also highlighted any gaps between filters and examination instructions and the credit's eligibility rules. We reviewed the filter results for tax year 2010 claims and interviewed SB/SE and TEGE officials about compliance efforts.

To assess what would be needed to evaluate the effects of credit, we conducted a literature review and interviewed representatives of the forenamed groups and subject matter specialists from government, academia, research foundations and think tanks. We selected the specialists based primarily on our literature review and spoke with individuals at the University of Massachusetts, Boston; Massachusetts Institute of Technology; the Commonwealth Fund; the Urban Institute; the Kaiser Family Foundation; the American Enterprise Institute; the Employee Benefit Research Institute; the RAND Corporation; the Small Business Administration Office of Advocacy; and the Office of Tax Policy at the Department of the Treasury. We reviewed available data in commonly cited surveys with questions on employer health insurance, and identified how the questions and variables match to the eligibility criteria for the credit.

We conducted this performance audit from July 2011 through May 2012 in accordance with generally accepted government auditing standards. Those standards require that we plan and perform the audit to obtain sufficient, appropriate evidence to provide a reasonable basis for our findings and conclusions based on our audit objectives. We believe that the evidence obtained provides a reasonable basis for our findings and conclusions based on our audit objectives.

APPENDIX II. STATE AVERAGE PREMIUMS FOR SMALL GROUP MARKETS FOR 2010 AND 2011

The Small Employer Health Insurance Tax Credit is based on a percentage of the lesser of (1) the premiums paid by the eligible small employer for employees during the taxable year and (2) the amount of premiums the employer would have paid if each employee were enrolled in a plan with a premium equal to the average premium for the small group market in the state (or in an area in the state) in which the employer is offering health insurance. The Secretary of Health and Human Services determines whether separate average premiums will apply for areas within a state and also determines the average premium for a state or substate area. Table 2 shows the average premiums for the small group market in each state for tax years 2010 and 2011.

Table 2. State Average Premiums for Small Group Markets for 2010 and 2011

	2010		2011	
	Employee only (single plan)	**Family plan**	**Employee only (single plan)**	**Family plan**
Alabama	$4,441	$11,275	$4,778	$12,084
Alaska	6,204	13,723	6,729	14,701
Arizona	4,495	10,239	4,614	11,063
Arkansas	4,329	9,677	4,378	9,849
California	4,628	10,957	4,790	11,493
Colorado	4,972	11,437	5,007	12,258
Connecticut	5,419	13,484	5,640	14,096
Delaware	5,602	12,513	5,902	13,411
District of Columbia	5,355	12,823	5,721	14,024
Florida	5,161	12,453	5,218	12,550
Georgia	4,612	10,598	5,085	11,440
Hawaii	4,228	10,508	4,622	11,529
Idaho	4,215	9,365	4,379	10,066
Illinois	5,198	12,309	5,565	13,176
Indiana	4,775	11,222	5,262	12,097
Iowa	4,652	10,503	4,694	11,051
Kansas	4,603	11,462	4,693	11,909
Kentucky	4,287	10,434	4,456	10,560
Louisiana	4,829	11,074	5,143	11,911
Maine	5,215	11,887	5,261	12,255
Maryland	4,837	11,939	5,073	12,530
Massachusetts	5,700	14,138	5,900	15,262
Michigan	5,098	12,364	5,195	12,539
Minnesota	4,704	11,938	5,048	12,790
Mississippi	4,533	10,501	4,787	10,860
Missouri	4,663	10,681	4,843	11,379
Montana	4,772	10,212	4,923	10,789
Nebraska	4,715	11,169	5,130	12,057
Nevada	4,553	10,297	4,781	10,836
New Hampshire	5,519	13,624	5,858	14,523
New Jersey	5,607	13,521	5,868	14,093
New Mexico	4,754	11,404	5,146	12,328
New York	5,442	12,867	5,589	13,631

	2010		2011	
	Employee only (single plan)	**Family plan**	**Employee only (single plan)**	**Family plan**
North Carolina	4,920	11,583	5,136	11,949
North Dakota	4,469	10,506	4,545	11,328
Ohio	4,667	11,293	4,706	11,627
Oklahoma	4,838	11,002	4,922	11,200
Oregon	4,681	10,890	4,881	11,536
Pennsylvania	5,039	12,471	5,186	12,671
Rhode Island	5,887	13,786	5,956	14,553
South Carolina	4,899	11,780	5,036	11,780
South Dakota	4,497	11,483	4,733	11,589
Tennessee	4,611	10,369	4,744	11,035
Texas	5,140	11,972	5,172	12,432
Utah	4,238	10,935	4,532	11,346
Vermont	5,244	11,748	5,426	12,505
Virginia	4,890	11,338	5,060	12,213
Washington	4,543	10,725	4,776	11,151
West Virginia	4,986	11,611	5,356	12,724
Wisconsin	5,222	12,819	5,284	13,911
Wyoming	5,266	12,163	5,430	12,867

Source: Department of Health and Human Services and IRS information.

APPENDIX III. ADJUSTMENTS IN COUNTING TOTAL SMALL EMPLOYER CLAIMS AND TOTAL CREDIT AMOUNT CLAIMS FOR TAX YEAR 2010

Internal Revenue Service (IRS) data for tax year 2010 show 335,600 total claims filed. This total must be adjusted to avoid counting the 110,800 S corporation and partnership claims that were passed through to 165,300 respective shareholders and partners who then filed their claims separately. Excluding the 165,300 shareholder and partner claims filed leaves 170,300 small employer claims filed. To capture the number of credit amounts claimed and avoid the amounts that were claimed by the S corporations and partnerships as well as their respective shareholders and partners, we excluded the 110,800 S corporation and partnership claims to arrive at 224,800 credit amounts claimed. (See figure 6.)

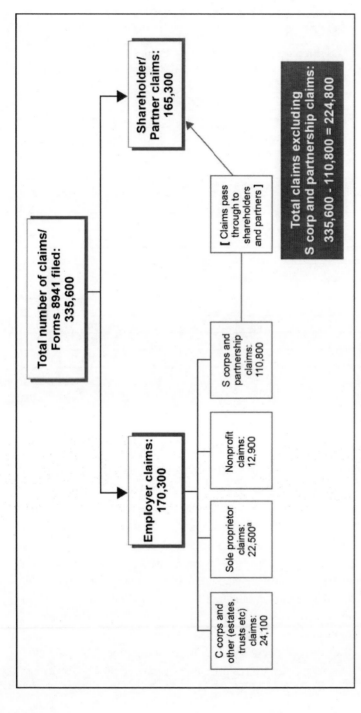

Source: GAO analysis of IRS data.

Note: Numbers rounded to the nearest hundred.

[a] Also included in this group are single member owners of disregarded limited liability corporations.

Figure 6. Number of Credit Claims by Taxpayer Type, Tax Year 2010.

APPENDIX IV. CREDIT CLAIMS BY EMPLOYER SIZE AND WAGES PAID, TAX YEAR 2010

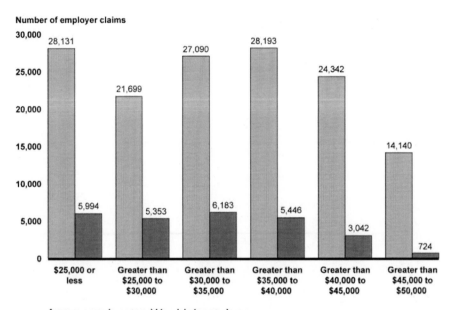

Number of employer claims

Source: GAO analysis of IRS data.

APPENDIX V. FORM 8941 AND WORKSHEETS FOR CLAIMING THE SMALL EMPLOYER HEALTH INSURANCE TAX CREDIT

This appendix contains Form 8941 and worksheets, shown in figure 4.

Form 8941

Department of the Treasury
Internal Revenue Service

Credit for Small Employer Health Insurance Premiums

▶ See separate instructions.
▶ Attach to your tax return.

OMB No. 1545-2198

2010

Attachment
Sequence No. 63

Name(s) shown on return

Identifying number

1	Enter the number of individuals you employed during the tax year who are considered employees for purposes of this credit (see instructions)	1	
2	Enter the number of full-time equivalent employees you had for the tax year (see instructions). If you entered 25 or more, skip lines 3 through 11 and enter -0- on line 12	2	
3	Average annual wages you paid for the tax year (see instructions). If you entered $50,000 or more, skip lines 4 through 11 and enter -0- on line 12	3	
4	Premiums you paid during the tax year for employees included on line 1 for health insurance coverage under a qualifying arrangement (see instructions)	4	
5	Premiums you would have entered on line 4 if the total premium for each employee equaled the average premium for the small group market in which you offered health insurance coverage (see instructions)	5	
6	Enter the **smaller** of line 4 or line 5	6	
7	Multiply line 6 by the applicable percentage: • Tax-exempt small employers, multiply line 6 by 25% (.25) • All other small employers, multiply line 6 by 35% (.35)	7	
8	If line 2 is 10 or less, enter the amount from line 7. Otherwise, see instructions	8	
9	If line 3 is $25,000 or less, enter the amount from line 8. Otherwise, see instructions	9	
10	Enter the total amount of any state premium subsidies paid and any state tax credits available to you for premiums included on line 4 (see instructions)	10	
11	Subtract line 10 from line 4. If zero or less, enter -0-	11	
12	Enter the **smaller** of line 9 or line 11	12	
13	If line 12 is zero, skip lines 13 and 14 and go to line 15. Otherwise, enter the number of employees included on line 1 for whom you paid premiums during the tax year for health insurance coverage under a qualifying arrangement (see instructions)	13	
14	Enter the number of full-time equivalent employees you would have entered on line 2 if you only included employees included on line 13	14	
15	Credit for small employer health insurance premiums from partnerships, S corporations, cooperatives, estates, and trusts (see instructions)	15	
16	Add lines 12 and 15. Partnerships and S corporations, stop here and report this amount on Schedule K; all others, go to line 17	16	
17	Credit for small employer health insurance premiums included on line 16 from passive activities (see instructions)	17	
18	Subtract line 17 from line 16	18	
19	Credit for small employer health insurance premiums allowed for 2010 from a passive activity (see instructions)	19	
20	Carryback of the credit for small employer health insurance premiums from 2011	20	
21	Add lines 18 through 20. Cooperatives, estates, and trusts, go to line 22. Tax-exempt small employers, skip lines 22 and 23 and go to line 24. All others, stop here and report this amount on Form 3800, line 29h	21	
22	Amount allocated to patrons of the cooperative or beneficiaries of the estate or trust (see instructions)	22	
23	Cooperatives, estates, and trusts, subtract line 22 from line 21. Stop here and report this amount on Form 3800, line 29h	23	
24	Enter the amount you paid in 2010 for taxes considered payroll taxes for purposes of this credit (see instructions)	24	
25	Tax-exempt small employers, enter the **smaller** of line 21 or line 24 here and on Form 990-T, line 44f	25	

For Paperwork Reduction Act Notice, see separate instructions.   Cat. No. 37757S   Form **8941** (2010)

Worksheet 1. Information Needed To Complete Line 1 and Worksheets 2 and 3

If you need more rows, use a separate sheet and include the additional amounts in the totals below.

	(a) Individuals Considered Employees	(b) Employee Hours of Service	(c) Employee Wages Paid
1.			
2.			
3.			
4.			
5.			
6.			
7.			
8.			
9.			
10.			
11.			
12.			
13.			
14.			
15.			
16.			
17.			
18.			
19.			
20.			
21.			
22.			
23.			
24.			
25.			
Totals:			

Worksheet 2. Full-Time Equivalent Employees (FTEs)

1. Enter the total employee hours of service from Worksheet 1, column (b) . . . . 1. _____
2. Hours of service per FTE . . . . 2. __2,080__
3. **Full-time equivalent employees.** Divide line 1 by line 2. If the result is not a whole number (0, 1, 2, etc.), generally round the result down to the next lowest whole number. However, if the result is less than one, enter 1. Report this amount on Form 8941, line 2 . . . . 3. _____

Worksheet 3. Average Annual Wages

1. Enter the total employee wages paid from Worksheet 1, column (c) . . . . 1. _____
2. Enter FTEs from Worksheet 2, line 3 . . . 2. _____
3. **Average annual wages.** Divide line 1 by line 2. If the result is not a multiple of $1,000 ($1,000, $2,000, $3,000, etc.), round the result down to the next lowest multiple of $1,000. Report this amount on Form 8941, line 3 . . . . 3. _____

Worksheet 4. Information Needed To Complete Lines 4 and 5 and Worksheet 7

If you need more rows, use a separate sheet and include the additional amounts in the totals below.

	(a) Enrolled Individuals Considered Employees	(b) Employer Premiums Paid	(c) Employer State Average Premiums	(d) Enrolled Employee Hours of Service
1.				
2.				
3.				
4.				
5.				
6.				
7.				
8.				
9.				
10.				
11.				
12.				
13.				
14.				
15.				
16.				
17.				
18.				
19.				
20.				
21.				
22.				
23.				
24.				
25.				
Totals:				

Worksheet 5. FTE Limitation

1. Enter the amount from Form 8941, line 7 . . 1. _____
2. Enter the amount from Form 8941, line 2 . . . . 2. _____
3. Subtract 10 from line 2 . . . . . . 3. _____
4. Divide line 3 by 15. Enter the result as a decimal (rounded to at least 3 places) . . . . 4. _____
5. Multiply line 1 by line 4 . . . . 5. _____
6. Subtract line 5 from line 1. Report this amount on Form 8941, line 8 . . . . 6. _____

Worksheet 6. Average Annual Wage Limitation

1. Enter the amount from Form 8941, line 8 . . . 1. _____
2. Enter the amount from Form 8941, line 7 . . . . 2. _____
3. Enter the amount from Form 8941, line 3 . . . . 3. _____
4. Subtract $25,000 from line 3 . . . . 4. _____
5. Divide line 4 by $25,000. Enter the result as a decimal (rounded to at least 3 places) . . . . 5. _____
6. Multiply line 2 by line 5 . . . . 6. _____
7. Subtract line 6 from line 1. Report this amount on Form 8941, line 9 . . . . 7. _____

Worksheet 7. FTEs Enrolled in Coverage

1. Enter the total enrolled employee hours of service from Worksheet 4, column (d) . . 1. _____
2. Hours of service per FTE . . . . 2. __2,080__
3. Divide line 1 by line 2. If the result is not a whole number (0, 1, 2, etc.), generally round the result down to the next lowest whole number. However, if the result is less than one, enter 1. Report this amount on Form 8941, line 14 . . . . 3. _____

Source: IRS.

APPENDIX VI. PUBLICALLY AVAILABLE DATA ON SMALL EMPLOYER HEALTH INSURANCE

Through our literature review and interviews, we identified several commonly cited non-Internal Revenue Service data sources on employer health insurance. Each source has different variables related to the key eligibility requirements for the Small Employer Health Insurance Tax Credit. Table 3 summarizes each source, its basic methodology, and whether its data matches with these requirements for the credit. The table only considers data that are readily accessible in public-use data sets.

Table 3. Publically Available Data on Small Employer Health Insurance

	Employer Health Benefits Survey	Medical Expenditure Panel Survey (Insurance Component)	National Compensation Survey
Sources and methodology			
Organizations responsible for the survey	Kaiser Family Foundation and Health Research and Educational Trust	Department of Health and Human Services, Agency for Healthcare Research and Quality	Bureau of Labor Statistics
Frequency and contact method	Annual, conducted by phone	Annual, generally conducted by phone or mail	Annual, conducted by personal visits, mail, telephone, and e-mail
Unit of analysis, sample size and source	Employers— 2,088 from Dun and Bradstreet and the Census of Governments	Employers[a]— 38,409 private sector establishments from U.S. Census Bureau's Business Register	Employers;[b] 15,566 private industry establishments from state unemployment insurance reports
Response rate and most recent data, as of April 2012	Forth-seven percent in 2011	Eighty-three percent for private establishments in 2010	Fifty-six percent for private industry in 2011
Key eligibility requirement for the credit, and whether the source contains data			
Employer is a for-profit or tax- exempt entity	Yes	Yes	Yes[c]

	Employer Health Benefits Survey	Medical Expenditure Panel Survey (Insurance Component)	National Compensation Survey
Employer offers health insurance and pays at least 50 percent of premiums	Yes	Yes	Yes
Employer has fewer than 25 full-time equivalents (FTE)	No— number of employees	No— number of employees	No— number of employees, from 1 to 49, and number of full- and part-time employees
Average annual wages are less than $50,000 per FTE	No— percentage of full-time employees who make $23,000 or less per year	No— percentage of employees who earned wages in one of three categories[d]	No— wages are presented in five percentiles[e]

Source: GAO analysis of data sources.

[a] The Medical Expenditure Panel Survey's Insurance Component sample is drawn at the establishment level; an establishment is a particular workplace or location.

[b] The National Compensation Survey sample is drawn at the establishment level; an establishment is a single economic unit that engages in one, or primarily one, type of economic activity. It is usually a single physical location.

[c] Statistical models used by the National Compensation Survey are able to control for profit/non-profit status.

[d] The annual wage categories are about (1) $23,920 or less, (2)$23,920 to $54,080, and (3) $54,080 or more.

[e] Wage data are presented in percentile categories in the published data. The annual wage categories, for private industry workers, are about: (1) 10th percentile makes $17,160 or less, (2) 25th percentile makes $22,235 or less, (3) 50th percentile makes $33,009 or less, (4) 75th percentile makes $51,605 or less, and (5) the 90th percentile makes $78,811 or less.

End Notes

[1] MEPS is a set of large-scale surveys. MEPS is administered by the Agency for Healthcare Research and Quality in the Department of Health and Human Services. The 2010 Insurance Component survey had a response rate of about 83 percent for private establishments, and 38,409 respondents, including for-profit, and nonprofit employers; government units are excluded from these statistics.

[2] Pub. L. No. 111-148, §§ 1421, 10105, 124 Stat. 119 (Mar. 23, 2010), (codified at 26 U.S.C. § 45R).

[3] CBO, letter to the Honorable Nancy Pelosi, Speaker of the U.S. House of Representatives (Washington, D.C.: Mar. 18, 2010).

[4] For example, see GAO, *Tax Refunds: Enhanced Prerefund Compliance Checks Could Yield Significant Benefits*, GAO-11-691T (Washington, D.C.: May 25, 2011).

[5] For additional description of challenges for small employers providing coverage, see GAO, *Private Health Insurance: Small Employers Continue to Face Challenges in Providing Coverage*, GAO-02-8 (Washington, D.C.: Oct. 31, 2001).

[6] In general, the federal minimum wage is $7.25 per hour. Many states also have minimum wage laws and minimum wages vary from state to state.

[7] See Quantria Strategies/Small Business Administration, *Health Insurance in the Small Business Market: Availability, Coverage, and the Effect of Tax Incentives* (Cheverly, Md.: September 2011).

[8] CBO estimated that for firms with 25 or fewer employees, 26 percent of premiums goes toward insurers' administration costs, compared with 7 percent for firms with at least 1,000 employees; see CBO, *Key Issues in Analyzing Major Health Insurance Proposals* (Washington, D.C.: December 2008).

[9] Risk pooling spreads risk across a group; a larger pool stabilizes the average insurance costs. Smaller risk pools raise costs because insurers run the risk of insuring those with relatively high health care needs. As a result, insurers may increase premiums to better ensure that they can cover unexpectedly large health care costs.

[10] The average deductible in 2010 per employee enrolled in a single (employee only) health insurance plan was $1,421 for employers with fewer than 10 employees; $1,420 for employers with 10 to 24 employees, $1,513 for employers with 25 to 99 employees, $1,155 for employers with 100 to 999 employees, and $738 for employers with 1,000 or more employees, according to MEPS. A deductible is the amount of expenses that must be paid out-of-pocket before an insurer will pay any expenses.

[11] For purposes of this credit, a business includes those that are corporations in a controlled group of corporations, or members of an affiliated service group, as well as partnerships, sole proprietorships, cooperatives and trusts. A sole proprietor is an individual who owns an unincorporated business but may employ others.

[12] The credit is available to tax-exempt employers described in 26 U.S.C. § 501(c) and exempt from tax under 26 U.S.C. § 501 (a).

[13] To calculate FTEs, the total hours of service must be determined for all individuals considered employees. There are a number of methods that can be used to determine the hours worked, but the hours are limited to 2,080 per employee. The total number of hours of service is divided by 2,080 to arrive at the FTE number.

[14] Other exclusions are seasonal employees, unless they work for the employer on more than 120 days in the tax year, and ministers who are deemed to be self-employed. Leased employees are included in FTE calculations.

[15] Wages for the employees included in the FTE calculations are included in average wage calculations except for minister's wages which are not subject to Social Security or Medicare tax.

[16] IRS offered a transition rule on the "qualifying arrangement" criteria for tax year 2010 and for satisfying the uniformity requirement. IRS Notice 2010-44.

[17] The unused credit for small businesses may be carried back 1 year or forward up to 20 years. Credits cannot be carried back to a year prior to the effective date of the credit; any unused credit amounts for 2010 can only be carried forward. See IRS Notice 2010-44.

[18] Owners of S corporations are referred to as shareholders. S corporations are corporations that "pass through" gains and losses to shareholders' individual tax returns without generally paying taxes at the entity level. Similarly, partners receive pass through income and losses from a partnership.

[19] For partners and shareholders, the credit is to be entered on the Schedule K-1 to be filed with an income tax return.

[20] PPACA requires the establishment of exchanges in each state by January 1, 2014, which are to help eligible individuals and small employers compare and select insurance coverage from among participating health plans. See Pub. L. No. 111-148, § 1311(b), 124 Stat. 119, 173 (Mar. 23, 2010).

[21] The number of employees who had their premiums paid by employers that claimed the credit was about 770,000.

[22] The Council of Economic Advisors is an agency within the Executive Office of the President charged with offering objective advice on the formulation of domestic and international economic policy, and SBA is a government agency that offers a variety of programs and support services to help small businesses.

[23] The estimate for SBM and SBA included nonprofits. The estimate for NFIB was only for small businesses; it is not known whether the estimate for the Council of Economic Advisors included nonprofits in addition to businesses.

[24] CBO and JCT recently reduced their original estimates of the future costs of the credit to a cost of $1 billion in 2012 and a cost of $21 billion from 2012 to 2021. These estimates were previously $5 billion in 2012 and $40 billion from 2012 to 2021.

[25] See app. IV for a graph of claimants with fewer than 10 FTEs and the amount of full credits.

[26] A small group plan is a health coverage plan sponsored by small employers for the employees.

[27] This MEPS statistic is based on employers—both profit and nonprofit—with fewer than 10 employees that pay annual wages of $24,000 or less to over half of their employees.

[28] This MEPS statistic is based on employers—both profit and nonprofit—with 10 to 25 employees that pay annual wages of $24,000 or less to over half of their employees. Because the employers eligible for the partial credit can pay up to $50,000 in wages, this is a less precise estimate than using MEPS to estimate insurance offerings for the full credit.

[29] The National Society of Accountants conducted a survey in 2008 that estimated the hourly tax preparer fee to be $122 an hour. Tax preparers may not necessarily charge for the credit, according to some discussion group participants.

[30] The Taxpayer Advocate Service is an independent organization within the IRS that helps taxpayers who are experiencing economic harm; are seeking help in resolving problems with IRS; and believe an IRS system or procedure is not working as it should.

[31] The NFIB Research Foundation is a nonprofit affiliated with NFIB.

[32] NFIB conducted this survey in April and May 2011 of 750 small employers of firms with 50 or fewer employees. The Kaiser Family Foundation conducted its survey from January through May 2011 of 3,184 public and private firms with 3 or more employees and its questions about the credit were directed to employers with 50 or fewer employees.

[33] Each focus group in 2011 consisted of 12 tax preparers. IRS issued a report on the focus groups' results on October 14, 2011.

[34] Given the previously discussed lack of knowledge or awareness, it is not clear that increasing outreach would increase credit usage.

[35] Three bills were recently introduced to amend the small employer health insurance credit to increase the maximum number of FTEs to 50, modify the phase out of the credit amount, and repeal the limitation based on state health insurance premium averages. H.R. 4324, Small Business Employee Health Insurance Credit Expansion Act of 2012, also would repeal the 2-year limit after 2014, making the credit available indefinitely. H.R.4252 and S.2227, both titled Small Business Health Care Tax Credit Improvement Act of 2012, propose to increase allowable average annual salaries paid to employees to $28,500 to claim the full credit.

[36] Using the number of employees instead of FTEs would require an increase in the number of eligible employees in order to reach the same population of small employers. For example, two part-time employees working 20 hours per week count as one FTE, making the employer appear larger than if FTEs were counted.

[37] We found that that IRS's compliance plans for the TETR were consistent with good management practices in previous reports. See GAO, *Tax Administration: Telephone Excise Tax Refund Requests Are Fewer Than Projected and Have Had Minimal Impact on IRS Services*, GAO-07-695 (Washington, D.C.: Apr. 11, 2007).

[38] We tested IRS's internal controls for the COBRA unemployment subsidies in the American Recovery and Reinvestment Act and found that IRS was able to identify all five fictitious companies used to fraudulently apply for the subsidies. See *GAO Proactive Testing of ARRA Tax Credits for COBRA Premium Payments*, GAO-10-804R (Washington, D.C.: June 14, 2010).

[39] See GAO, *Tax Gap: Complexity and Taxpayer Compliance*, GAO-11-747T (Washington, D.C.: June 28, 2011).

[40] The Internal Revenue Code provides IRS with MEA to assess additional tax or otherwise correct tax return errors in limited circumstances when an adjustment is the result of mathematical or clerical errors on the return. In these cases, IRS can avoid costly audits and IRS is not required to provide taxpayers a right to appeal MEA assessments, although they may file a claim to ask IRS to reduce the assessment if they believe IRS erred. See 26 U.S.C. § 6213(b). Over the years, Congress has granted MEA for specific purposes and those purposes are listed in section 6213(g)(2).

[41] These three IRS filters are to check whether credit claims are consistent with eligibility requirements subject to computation criteria.

[42] We previously recommended that Congress should consider broadening IRS s ability to use MEA, with appropriate safeguards against misuse. See GAO, *Recovery Act: IRS Quickly Implemented Tax Provisions, but Reporting and Enforcement Improvements Are Needed*, GAO-10-349 (Washington, D.C.: Feb. 10, 2010).

[43] We do not describe the filters and the eligibility requirements not being covered in detail because of concerns about revealing IRS's compliance approach and criteria.

[44] See 26 U.S.C. § 6051(a)(14), which generally requires employers to report the aggregate cost of employer-sponsored coverage they provide for an employee on Form W-2.

[45] TEGE established two mandatory filters that if failed, automatically trigger an exam; only 16 forms tripped these two filters, as of December 31, 2011.

[46] Examiner instructions consist of several types of documents, such as worksheets and checklists on the credit's eligibility requirements; we also refer to these documents as examination "guidance."

[47] Tax-exempt entities with non-U.S. addresses must pay health insurance premiums for an employee's coverage issued in and regulated in one of the states or the District of Columbia.

[48] TEGE examinations will only cover the credit, according to IRS officials.

[49] A soft notice is a letter generated to taxpayers that IRS has identified possible errors on the taxpayer's form. The goal is to increase compliance at minimal costs by educating taxpayers for future compliance without doing an examination and minimizing the taxpayers' need to respond to the notice.

[50] For example, see GAO, *Advance Earned Income Tax Credit: Low Use and Small Dollars Paid Impede IRS's Efforts to Reduce High Noncompliance*, GAO-07-1110 (Washington, D.C.: Aug. 10, 2007), and *Tax Gap: IRS Could Do More to Promote Compliance by Third Parties with Miscellaneous Income Reporting Requirements*, GAO-09 -238 (Washington, D.C.: Jan. 28, 2009).

[51] For details on methods for identifying causation, including experiments and quasi-experiments, using comparison groups, see GAO, *Designing Evaluations: 2012 Revision*, GAO-12 -208G (Washington, D.C.: January 2012). These designs are not feasible for the credit because it was implemented simultaneously across the country.

[52] See GAO, *Government Performance and Accountability: Tax Expenditures Represent a Substantial Federal Commitment and Need to Be Reexamined*, GAO-05-690 (Washington, D.C.: Sept. 23, 2005).

[53] Starting in 2014, eligible small employers can claim the credit for the 2 consecutive years beginning when the employer first offers employee health insurance from a state exchange.

[54] TIGTA, *Affordable Care Act: Efforts to Implement the Small Business Health Care Tax Credit Were Mostly Successful, but Some Improvements Are Needed*, 2011-40-103 (Washington, D.C.: Sept. 19, 2011).

[55] For example, see GAO, *Tax Refunds: Enhanced Prerefund Compliance Checks Could Yield Significant Benefits*, GAO-11-691T (Washington, D.C.: May 25, 2011).

INDEX